D1275439

Microsoft®
Expression® Web Plain & Simple

Katherine Murray

PUBLISHED BY
Microsoft Press
A Division of Microsoft Corporation
One Microsoft Way
Redmond, Washington 98052-6399

Library of Congress Control Number: 2007934743

Printed and bound in the United States of America.

1 2 3 4 5 6 7 8 9   QWT   2 1 0 9 8 7

Distributed in Canada by H.B. Fenn and Company Ltd.

A CIP catalogue record for this book is available from the British Library.

Microsoft Press books are available through booksellers and distributors worldwide. For further information about international editions, contact your local Microsoft Corporation office or contact Microsoft Press International directly at fax (425) 936-7329. Visit our Web site at www.microsoft.com/mspress. Send comments to mspinput@microsoft.com.

Microsoft, Microsoft Press, Excel, Expression, Expression Blend, FrontPage, Georgia, PowerPoint, SharePoint, Verdana, Visual Studio, Windows, Windows Live, and Windows Vista are either registered trademarks or trademarks of Microsoft Corporation in the United States and/or other countries. Other product and company names mentioned herein may be the trademarks of their respective owners.

The example companies, organizations, products, domain names, e-mail addresses, logos, people, places, and events depicted herein are fictitious. No association with any real company, organization, product, domain name, e-mail address, logo, person, place, or event is intended or should be inferred.

This book expresses the author's views and opinions. The information contained in this book is provided without any express, statutory, or implied warranties. Neither the authors, Microsoft Corporation, nor its resellers, or distributors will be held liable for any damages caused or alleged to be caused either directly or indirectly by this book.

Acquisitions Editor: Juliana Aldous Atkinson
Developmental Editor: Sandra Haynes
Project Editor: Kathleen Atkins
Editorial Production: Abshier House
Technical Reviewer: James Lissiak; Technical Review services provided by Content Master, a member of CM Group, Ltd.
Cover Design: Tom Draper Design

Body Part No. X14-06993

Contents

What do you think of this book? We want to hear from you!

Microsoft is interested in hearing your feedback so we can continually improve our books and learning resources for you. To participate in a brief online survey, please visit:

www.microsoft.com/learning/booksurvey/

4 Working with Pages 39

5 Adding and Editing Text 55

6 Working with Pictures 85

7 Creating Links 109

8 Adding Tables   129

9 Working with Frames   149

13 Publishing Your Site   217

14 Creating Site Reports   229

What do you think of this book? We want to hear from you!

Microsoft is interested in hearing your feedback so we can continually improve our books and learning resources for you. To participate in a brief online survey, please visit:

www.microsoft.com/learning/booksurvey/

viii Contents

Acknowledgments

Every book is really a mix of talents and voices and abilities, and that's what I love about publishing. You have a whole group of people around you as you begin to create your first web page with Expression Web, and each person had an important part to play. Big thanks go to

- Juliana Aldous Atkinson, Microsoft Press Acquisitions Editor extraordinaire, for loving the idea for this book and whole-heartedly wanting to publish it,

- Claudette Moore, my agent, for making things happen in such a wonderful and always supportive way,

- Sandra Haynes, for spearheading this project initially, offering feedback, and lots of encouragement,

- Kathleen Atkins, project editor, for managing everything so well and keeping things flowing (quickly!),

- Nan Brooks, copy editor, for doing such a good job of catching the goofs, cleaning up phrases, and making sure everything reads well,

- Joell Smith-Borne, project editor, for her tireless work in overseeing the project and keeping us faithful to the conventions,

- James Lissiak, technical editor, for going so carefully through every line of the manuscript and offering suggestions and tips,

- Debbie Berman, compositor, who may have spent as much time with this book as I did, pouring her heart and considerable design talent into the beautiful pages you see today,

- Debbie Abshier, of Abshier House, for her experience, humor, kindness, and in-the-trenches knowledge—and, last in the process, but not in any way least,

- Kelly Quirino, proofreader, for a heroic, high-pressure proofreading pass, done almost at the very last moment!

I enjoyed working with all of you and hope we will work together on another book soon!

Dedication

To Mike Reeds, because he's the one who suggested I write a book about this great program, and

For my Dad, because he would have had a *blast* with Expression Web. We miss you Pop.

Jack Hawthorne
June 1932–April 2007

1 About This Book

At last! Web design for the rest of us.

Over the last 10 years or so, you've probably noticed the Web exploding all around you. You may have tried your hand at creating a few sites. Perhaps you even learned your way around Microsoft FrontPage and figured out enough about Web design to hang a shingle on the Web.

In the early days of the Web, sites consisted of mostly text and hyperlinks with a few pictures scattered here and there. The text was usually displayed as bulleted lists or long paragraphs; the images were cartoonish graphics with a few photos thrown in for extra impact. Today's Web is a dramatic improvement over the limited capabilities of the early days—now in addition to text, you find streaming video, sound, high-quality photos, color, chat, podcasts, calendars, interactive forms, and just about anything else you can imagine.

You might think that creating one of these media-rich sites would be a challenge way beyond the capabilities of a beginning Web designer, but if you've got the right tool, you're halfway there.

And the right tool, of course, is Microsoft Expression Web.

Microsoft Expression Web is Microsoft's answer to the next generation of feature-rich, standards-based Web design. Using Expression Web, you can create anything from simple, no-nonsense Web sites to sophisticated sites that make the most of a variety of media, include e-commerce features, interact with databases, and much more. Whether you are an experienced professional Web designer or someone who is just getting started designing your first site, Microsoft Expression Web gives you a full set of powerful tools and the support to help you plan, design, create, enhance, and publish sites that naturally conform to today's Web standards.

What Happened to Microsoft FrontPage?

Microsoft FrontPage has been Microsoft's Web design product for almost a decade, but today's Web calls for a new set of tools. FrontPage was a great product in its own right, enabling designers to produce top-quality sites of all kinds, but FrontPage has been discontinued and will not be going through any future revisions. Microsoft Expression Web includes and extends the best features of FrontPage for the professional Web designer. For Web professionals working with SharePoint sites, Microsoft now offers Microsoft Office SharePoint Designer 2007, and for Web developers working with ASP.NET, Microsoft suggests Microsoft Visual Studio 2005.

What You'll Find Here

Microsoft Expression Web Plain & Simple is the book for you if you want to learn—without a lot of fuss and fanfare—how to create great Web sites using Microsoft Expression Web. The format is full-color, informative, and clear: you can find what you need easily and put the steps directly into practice. That's the best way to learn anyway.

Each section covers a different aspect of Web page creation, arranged in a logical sequence so that you can follow along reading one right after another if that's your style. But don't feel limited by the format—if you prefer to pick and choose your topic, skipping around in the book to read only what you need, by all means do that! Each section is presented in a series of short (two-page) tasks, so you can easily jump from item to item as your interest dictates.

Section 2 introduces you to the lay of the land. You'll find out how to start Microsoft Expression Web, find your way around the screen, explore the tools, display different views, use shortcut keys, and get help when you need it.

Section 3 is all about creating that first Web site. In this chapter, you learn how to plan your new site and then create it. You'll find out about various ways to create the site: starting with a blank page, using a template, or importing an existing site. Once you have created your site, you learn how to track site information and set your Web preferences.

Section 4 focuses on the individual Web page—one page of your overall site. In this section, you learn how to manage your pages (by opening, renaming, saving, and deleting them), as well as how to decorate the page background, preview your pages, and use Dynamic Web Templates to automate page generation for pages that will share common elements.

Sections 5 and 6 are all about the content. Here you learn how to add text and pictures to your Web pages and enhance them using a variety of simple techniques: create bullet lists, change font and format, tweak the alignment, do simple editing, run the spelling checker (don't forget!), and control text wrap around images. It's all pretty straightforward, wrapped up nice and neat in these two key sections.

Section 7 shines a spotlight on the prima donna of the Web page: the link. The Web wouldn't exist without what we once called the *hyperlink*—the hot spot on your page (text, image, or button) that users click to move from one page to another. This section shows you how to add links to any and all elements on your page, and shows you how to troubleshoot and repair them when they don't seem to be working properly.

Section 8 will be a treat for those of you who like your information organized and neatly structured because it shows you how to create tables for your pages. Knowing how to create a table for your Web page is a great tool to have in your designer's toolkit. Tables enable you to create a structure for information that gives it boundaries, which is a nice thing when you are designing a page that will be viewed by people all over the world with all sorts of different Web browsers.

Sections 9 and 10 walk you through the steps for creating frames and forms, two elements that you may use only once in a while in your Web design work (depending on your own preferences and the data needs of your client or organization). These sections show you how to create, resize, split, and enhance frames and add and customize form controls on your pages.

Section 11 gets right to the heart of high-energy site design by showing you how to add interactivity to your Web sites. In this section you learn all about behaviors, actions, and events (which do just what they sound like they do). You also find out how to add behaviors to specific elements on your page and control what they do when users click them. This chapter also shows you how to add sounds to your page, expanding your site visitors' experience into a new dimension.

Section 12 is all about our old friend CSS (Cascading Style Sheets), introducing you to the basics of CSS and showing you how to create, attach, and work with a style sheet as you design new pages. You'll also find out about layering and working with XML in Expression Web. The tasks covered here aren't too complex—nothing in this book is, or the name *Plain*

& Simple wouldn't apply—but unless you're an experienced Web designer, this probably isn't the first chapter you want to read.

Sections 13 and 14 put the finishing touches on the whole Web design process. Here you learn how to publish your site to the Web. What exactly does that mean, and how do you know you're ready to do it? You learn how to publish the site from your local PC and from a remote server; you'll get a list of troubleshooting ideas so you can sidestep any potential trouble spots or resolve them before they show up. Then, once your site is published, you find out how to create reports that tell you who is visiting your site, how often, and where they're coming from—all important information if you're interested in increasing your site traffic and making the most of your ability to publish online.

A Little About You

You were a really important part of the planning of this book. We wondered about you—what do you most need to know? Which programs are you most familiar with? What is your comfort level with computers? We know you surf the Web, but have you designed pages for it? How can we best help you get what you want from this book?

Microsoft Expression Web Plain & Simple was written with certain assumptions in mind. First, we assume that you want to begin using Microsoft Expression Web right away to create Web sites that will grow with you over the long haul. It's a big, complex program, but the developers have gone to great lengths to make the features easy to understand and use. So if you want to learn the basics of creating, enhancing, and publishing your first site in Microsoft Expression Web—and you want to do it quickly and easily—you'll find what you're looking for in these pages.

Microsoft is promoting Microsoft Expression Web as the tool of choice for the professional Web designer. This may leave you wondering, "Am I a Web designer?" We assume that you are just beginning to use Microsoft Expression Web but you are familiar with some of the basics of Web design. Perhaps you are standing in the bookstore right now, leafing through the pages of this book, wondering whether Microsoft Expression Web is the product (and, by extension, whether this is the book) that will help you create the kind of Web site you envision. Is it worth the investment?

Let us make the answer easy for you: If you (1) have a real interest in Web design and want to learn how to do it well; (2) plan to create more than just one site (something fun as a hobby or as a favor for a family member or friend); and (3) want to learn the basics of designing standards-based sites so your knowledge will serve as a foundation for other areas you want to explore in Web design (for example, creating content or developing Web solutions), spending a couple of afternoons learning Microsoft Expression Web is a good investment of your time.

A Little About the Microsoft Expression Suite

The Microsoft Expression Suite is a collection of Web tools designed for Web professionals. The products were new (available in beta, or public testing, format) in 2006, and are now available in wide release. Microsoft Expression Suite includes the following programs:

- Microsoft Expression Web, for creating professional, standards-based Web sites
- Microsoft Expression Blend, for designing engaging user experiences
- Microsoft Expression Design, for producing high-quality illustrations
- Microsoft Expression Media, for expert management of media files

The entire suite is available for purchase now, and each of the products can be purchased individually. You can also download a free trial of each of the programs, which enables you to try the product before you buy. To find out more about the programs in the Microsoft Expression Suite, visit *www.microsoft.com/Expression*.

A Quick Look Ahead

Now that you've got the basic plan for the path in front of you, are you ready to get started? Bring your creative ideas, a little free time, and some good old-fashioned inspiration, and let's create that first Web site with Microsoft Expression Web.

Getting Started with Expression Web

In this section:

- Starting Expression Web
- Checking Out the Workspace
- Choosing Your Tools
- Getting Familiar with the Editing Window
- Using Task Panes
- Reading the Status Bar
- Displaying Different Views
- Getting Help When You Need It

The first step in learning any new program involves finding out where everything is—and that's a good place to start with Expression Web. The opening window may leave you scratching your head and wondering where to begin, but after you finish reading this section, you'll know where to find the tools you need and be ready to focus your creative energy and get busy creating your first site.

Expression Web often gives you more than one way to do a specific task. You will work with views, task panes, shortcut keys, and more as you begin to build and publish your sites. This section introduces you to the Expression Web workspace and shows you where to find everything you need to get going.

Starting Expression Web

Launching Expression Web is similar whether you're using Windows XP or Windows Vista. The first time you open the program, you'll most likely begin with the Start button, but you can also create a desktop shortcut for Expression Web if you're going to use the program regularly and you'd rather skip the whole point-and-click menu thing.

Start the Program

1. Click the Start button or press the Windows key on your keyboard and click All Programs.

2. Scroll through the list and click the Microsoft Expression folder.

3. Click Microsoft Expression Web.

Tip ✓

Want a faster way? You can add a Microsoft Expression Web shortcut to your desktop by right-clicking anywhere on the desktop, pointing to New, and clicking Shortcut. In the Create Shortcut window, click Browse and navigate to the Microsoft Expression folder (in the Program Files folder). Click Next, and click Finish. The shortcut is now on your desktop, and you can start the program at any time by double-clicking it.

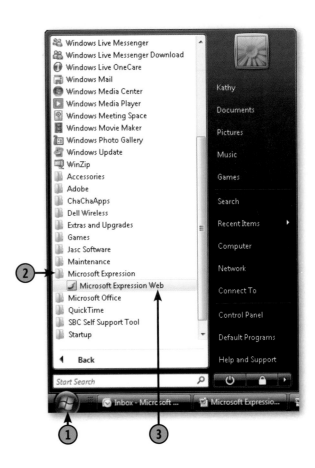

Checking Out the Workspace

When you start Microsoft Expression Web for the first time—especially if you are new to Web design—you may get a sinking feeling and wonder whether you'll ever find your way around the program. Don't worry—you will. Once you learn where everything is, finding your way around the workspace and choosing the tools you need becomes second nature. You can take some comfort in the fact that finding your way around Expression Web is *much* easier than it is in other Web tools popular today!

Tip

You can easily rearrange items in the Microsoft Expression Web workspace. You might, for example, drag the different task panes around, layer them, or create more space for the editing window. When you want to go back to the way Expression Web looked when you first started it, click the Task Panes menu, then click Reset Workspace Layout.

Menu bar   Editing window   Searchable help

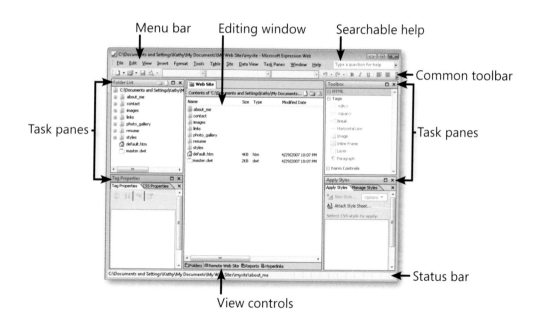

Common toolbar

Task panes

Task panes

Status bar

View controls

Choosing Your Tools

Microsoft Expression Web gives you a number of different menus related to specific steps you'll follow as you design and create Web sites. Some of the commands in the menus have corresponding buttons on the Common toolbar so that you can use them without having to open a menu to find and select them.

Tip

You'll notice when you begin to explore the different menus that the Common toolbar brings together the most commonly used tools in both the Standard and Formatting toolbars.

Meet the Menus in Expression Web

File	Start a new site; add a page; open, import, export, save, preview, and publish sites; exit the program.
Edit	Cut, copy, and paste page elements; find and replace page elements; check pages in and out; use the code editor.
View	Change the page view; display formatting marks and visual aids; control the ruler and grid; change page size; display and hide toolbars; refresh the display.
Insert	Add HTML tags, ASP.NET controls, pictures, bookmarks, links, files, buttons, and symbols.
Format	Attach style sheets, work with styles and properties, apply Dynamic Web Templates and Master Pages, control formatting for fonts and paragraphs, apply borders and shading, choose positioning, set the page background, control behaviors, work with frames, and remove formatting.
Tools	Use the spelling checker and thesaurus, set language options, produce accessibility and compatibility reports, work with macros and add-ins, customize application and page editor options.
Table	Insert, delete, and modify tables; work with layout tables; convert and fill tables; change table properties.
Site	Create and manage site folders, work with remote sites, produce site reports, manage hyperlinks, change site settings.
Data View	Display data view, work with data sources, edit data, sort and filter data, apply conditional formatting, refresh data view, control data view properties.
Task Panes	Choose to display or hide various task panes; reset the workspace layout to its original display.
Window	Move among open windows in Expression Web.
Help	Use Expression Web help; visit the online community; access additional Express Web resources.

Work with Menus

(1) Click the menu name in the menu bar.

(2) Do one of the following:

- Point to a command with an arrow to display more choices.

- Click a command to select it.

- Press the shortcut keys displayed to the right of the command.

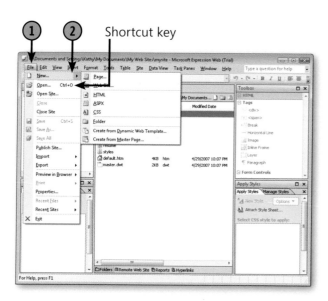

Use Shortcut Keys

Because Expression Web is a Microsoft product, many of the same shortcut keys you use in other Microsoft programs also work in Expression Web. Nice and convenient. If you use any Microsoft Office program, the shortcut keys for working with files (including Ctrl+P for print, Ctrl+O for opening a file, Ctrl+N to start a new file, and Ctrl+S to save); for toggling between open windows (Ctrl+Tab and Ctrl+Shift+Tab); and for undoing and redoing actions (Ctrl+Z and Ctrl+Y) will all be familiar. In addition to these kinds of "global" shortcut keys, Expression Web includes a number of keys you may want to use to speed up everyday tasks:

Expression Web Shortcuts—Fast Favorites

Shortcut Key	Purpose
F5	Refresh the current Editing window.
Ctrl+page Down or Ctrl+page Up	Move among Design, Split, and Code views.
Alt+F1	Hide and, alternately, show the Folders List.
Ctrl+Q	Display the Quick Tag Editor.
Ctrl+G	Go to a specific line, in Code view; Go to a specific bookmark, in Design view.
Ctrl+shift+: (colon)	Select the current tag and its contents.
Ctrl+; (semicolon)	Find the matching open or closing tag.

 Tip

This is only a sampling of the variety of shortcut keys that are available in Expression Web. You'll find out more about shortcut keys in the sections related to the functions they perform.

Check Out the Common Toolbar

When you first start Expression Web, only the Common toolbar is displayed. This toolbar includes command buttons you use for creating, enhancing, and working with Web pages.

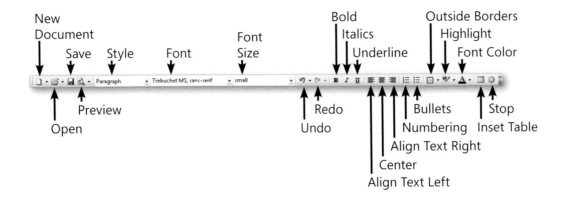

Tip

As your experience with Expression Web grows, you may find that you use certain tools regularly in your work and others, not so much. You can easily create your own custom toolbar with only your favorite tools by clicking the View menu, pointing to Toolbars, then clicking Customize. In the Customize dialog box, use the Toolbars tab to create a new toolbar and then use the Commands tab to add the commands you want to the toolbar you created. (If you want to get to the Customize dialog box even faster, click the arrow at the end of the Common toolbar, point to Add Or Remove Buttons, and click Customize.)

Try This!

There are so many tools available on the Common toolbar that, depending on your screen resolution, they may not all be displayed at one time. If there are any tools tucked away out of sight, a chevron [>>] will appear in the top right corner of the Common toolbar. When you click it, a small palette of tools appears. Click the one you want to use, and it will be added to the toolbar (and another one you haven't used yet—or you use rarely—will be moved to the palette).

Know Your Toolbar

Toolbar	Purpose
Standard	Shares a number of tools with the Common toolbar, providing you with the tools you need for creating and working with Web pages, as well as tools for previewing, publishing, and printing your Web pages.
Formatting	Also shares tools with the Common toolbar, and provides tools for managing styles and formatting text on your Web pages.
Code View	Gives you tools for working directly with the code of your pages—includes tools for working with tags, bookmarks, and links.
Common	Brings you the most common tools used in creating and modifying Web pages.
Dynamic Web Template	Displays a small toolbar with special tools for modifying and updating Web pages you create using Dynamic Web Templates.
Master Page	Shows a small toolbar with specific tools for working with Master Pages, enabling you to select and edit content regions on your Web pages.
Pictures	Provides tools for inserting, editing, and creating links for images on your Web pages.
Positioning	Gives you the ability to provide specific positioning values for an element on your Web page.
Style	Displays a small toolbar with tools for selecting styles in a particular class and ID category, creating a new style, and attaching a style sheet.
Style Applications	Enables you to choose how a particular style will be applied on the current Web page.
Tables	Provides you with tools for everything you might want to do with a table—create, modify, expand, color, and align text—and includes tools for creating and working with layout tables.

Getting Familiar with the Editing Window

The Editing window is the place where all the fun stuff happens—it's where you'll create, enhance, and modify your Web pages. When you first start Expression Web, the Editing window displays the Web Site tab, listing the folders and files in the current site. When you begin working on a page, the page and all its elements appear in the Editing window. Along the side of the Editing window, task panes provide you with tools for working with the page in various ways. At the bottom of the Editing window you'll find the View controls, each of which provides you with a different way of viewing your Web site.

Explore the Editing Window

① Double-click default.htm in the Folder List, to the left of the Editing window. Notice that the page opens in a new tab in the Editing window.

② Drag the vertical scrollbar on the right side of the Editing window to scroll through the page. Return to the top of the page.

③ Click in the paragraph text of the sample page. Notice the Content and P tabs that appear at the top of the paragraph. The Quick Tag Selector bar displays the HTML tags that are applied to the element you clicked.

④ Continue clicking other items on the page and notice the change in the Quick Tag Selector bar. For example, you may want to select the image, headings, and links on the page.

Quick Tag Selector bar

Tip

Expression Web automatically opens the most recently used Web site when you start the program. If you are starting the program for the first time and no example files appear in the Folder List, open the File menu, point to New, and click Web Site. In the New dialog box, click Templates and then select any template in the list that appeals to you. Click OK to open a new site based on that that template. You can use the new site as you learn about the Editing window in the next section.

Using Task Panes

Task panes will be your best friends as you work with Expression Web. They surround the editing window, placing within your easy reach the tools and options you need to build, modify, and fine-tune your pages. Each task pane offers a specific set of tools related to one aspect of creating a page or site. When you first start Microsoft Expression Web, the Folder List, Tag Properties, Toolbox, and Apply Styles task panes appear (because these are the most commonly used), but which task panes you display—and how many—is totally up to you. You will find more task panes in the Task Panes menu. As you get accustomed to working with Expression Web, you'll develop a feel for which task panes to use when.

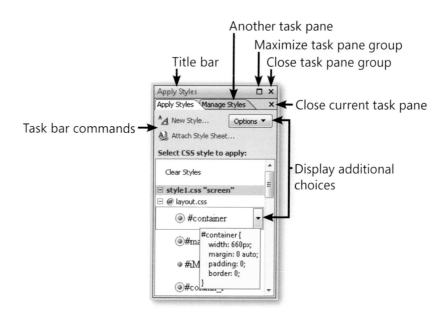

Another task pane
Maximize task pane group
Close task pane group
Title bar
Close current task pane
Task bar commands
Display additional choices

Expression Web Task Panes

Task Pane	Purpose
Folder List	Provides access to all elements—folders, files, pages—in your Web site.
Tag Properties	Enables you to see and modify the properties of tags on the current page.
CSS Properties	Enables you to view and work with the properties of CSS styles on the current page.
Layout Tables	Gives you tools to add a custom or predesigned layout table to your page.
Apply Styles	Displays CSS styles available in the current page and enables you to select, change, view, or remove styles; change all styles; and attach and remove style sheets.
Manage Styles	Enables you to view all styles in the current document and work with them in various ways. Additionally, you can move styles to different style sheets using this task pane.
Behaviors	Provides you with options for adding and fine-tuning a behavior to an element on the current Web page.
Layers	Displays a list of all the layers that are used in the current Web page so that you can reorder, modify, add, or remove layers.
Toolbox	Provides a set of common HTML tools and form controls, as well as ASP.NET tools.
Data Source Library	Enables you to attach a data source to your site (for example, when you are working with XML or building an ASP.NET site).
Data Source Details	Shows information about any data sources currently attached to the selected page.
Conditional Formatting	Enables you to apply conditional formatting to selected text, HTML tags, or data values in the current page.
Find 1 and Find 2	Two Find task panes that enable you to search for and replace elements in the current page or throughout the site. You can also perform saved queries using Find 1 and Find 2.
Accessibility	Enables you to run the Accessibility Checker and resolve issues found on the current page or throughout the site.
Compatibility	Lets you run the Compatibility Checker and identify and resolve problems related to HTML and CSS standards.
Hyperlinks	Displays and verifies all hyperlinks on the current page and enables you to correct link problems.
CSS Reports	Enables you to create CSS Reports showing both usage and error information related to the current page.

Rearrange Task Panes

① Click the Toolbox title bar and drag it to the center of the workspace. The task pane floats on top of the workspace.

② Click the Apply Styles title bar and drag it to a task pane on the other side of the workspace and release it.

③ Right-click the Toolbox title bar and click Dock. The task pane returns to its original position.

④ Click the Close Window button in the right corner of the Apply Styles task pane.

⑤ Open the Task Panes menu and click Reset Workspace Layout to put everything back the way you found it.

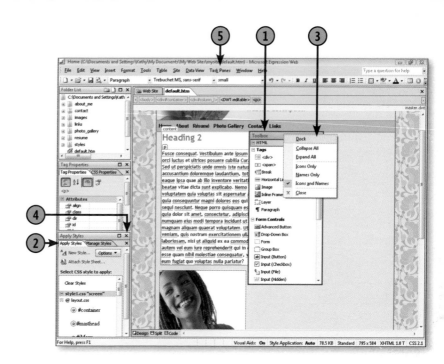

Tip ✓

If you're having trouble getting a task pane to float, right-click the task pane tab and click Float.

Tip ✓

Expression Web remembers the layout of the workspace, so the next time you start the program, the task panes will be arranged just the way you left them.

Reading the Status Bar

The status bar in Expression Web offers suggestions related to the task at hand. When you click an image in the Editing window, for example, the status bar displays a suggestion for resizing the margins of the image. On the right side of the status bar, you'll find a number of indicators that provide good-to-know information about your current file.

Read the Status Bar

- The left side of the status bar gives you information about ways you can work with the selected item on the page.

- The Visual Aids indicator lets you know that visual aids are currently turned on, helping you see which tags and elements are at work on your page. (The content tab you saw earlier in this chapter was one of Expression Web's Block Selection visual aids.)

- Style Application shows you that the mode is set to Auto. The Style Application mode determines whether a style on your page is applied automatically or manually.

- Download Statistics gives you information about the HTML, links, number of files, and total download size of the current page.

- The Rendering Mode indicator shows that the Web site is using standards compliant rendering. This setting is controlled by the Doctype of the page.

- Page Size displays the size, in pixels, of the current page.

- The Schema indicator (XHTML 1.0) shows that the HTML/XHTML schema is being used for the current page.

- The CSS Indicator shows the version of the CSS schema that is being used for the current page.

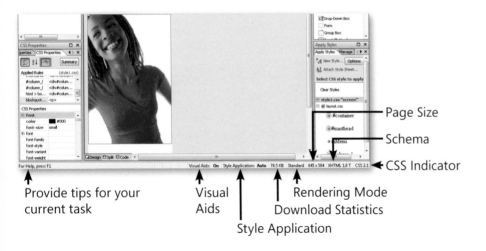

Page Size
Schema
CSS Indicator

Provide tips for your current task
Visual Aids
Style Application
Rendering Mode
Download Statistics

Tip

You can change most of the items directly on the status by double-clicking the indicator and making your selections in the dialog box or menu that appears.

Displaying Different Views

Once you know the lay of the land, you begin to see that Expression Web is a smart, powerful program that brings just what you need within reach. As you begin to build your own Web sites, you will want to be able to see the code you're creating (even if you're not working at a code level)

and preview the page to see how it will look in various Web browsers. Expression Web offers three different views you can use to see different aspects of your Web page: Design view, Split view, and Code view.

Three Perspectives, One Page

Design view is the default view, showing you the header, text, and images on your page in a manner close to what visitors will see when they visit your page.

Split view displays two windows in one, showing you Design view in a pane at the bottom of the Editing window and Code view in a pane at the top. Split view is great for those times when you want to find and modify or replace an element on your page. It also enables you to see changes in the code or watch for potential code problems.

Code view shows the code behind the display and layout of your document, enabling you to read through the code quickly, search and replace elements or tags, copy and paste sections, and more.

Use Split View

1. With the sample Web site open in Expression Web, click Split at the bottom of the Editing window.

2. Click the handle in the scroll bar in the top pane and drag it down until <h2>Heading</h2> appears in the top pane.

3. Click inside the <h2> tag.

4. Notice that Heading 2 is highlighted in the bottom pane of the Editing window.

Tip

Visual Aids used to help you learn and understand the elements while you're working in Design view may change the display just a bit. To get a true sense of how the page will look in a browser, turn off Visual Aids by double-clicking Visual Aids in the status bar.

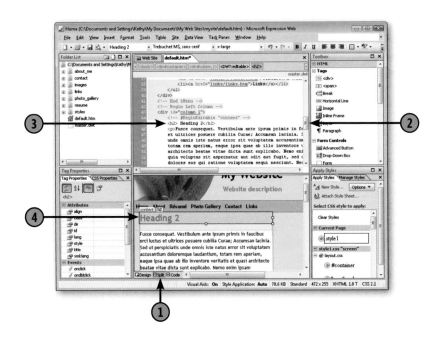

Getting Help When You Need It

Expression Web has a good help system that provides detailed information about the different tasks you'll be carrying out. If you've used any Microsoft product before, you will recognize the Help box in the upper right corner of the Expression Web window. You can get help several ways:

① Press F1 at any time to display help content related to the task you're performing.

② Type a word or phrase in the Help box to display Help content related to that topic.

③ Open the Help menu and click Microsoft Expression Web Help to display the Help system.

④ Open the Help menu and click Community to go online to a community of Expression Web users and Microsoft Most Valuable Professionals (MVPs), where you can search for answers and post questions for the group.

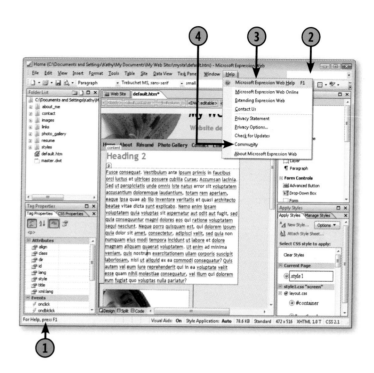

Use the Help System

1. Press F1 to display the Expression Web Help window.

2. Click the category you want to know more about.

3. Click the subcategory related to the specific task you are trying to complete.

4. Review the information, and click any additional links that are relevant to your task.

5. Click the Keep On Top icon if you want to be able to refer to this information as you work.

6. When you're finished with Help, click the Close box.

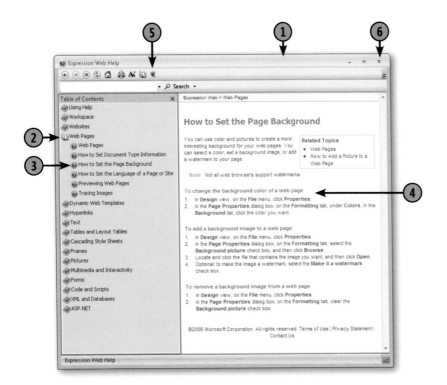

See Also

The Expression Web home page includes a Knowledge Center link that takes you to a number of tutorials and video segments on Expression Web. Go to *www.microsoft.com/expression* to find out more.

Tip

In the top left corner of the Help window, you can also click in the Search box and type a word or phrase related to the topic you want to know more about. The panel on the right side of the Help window displays links to more information about the topic. Click the link to find the information you want.

Moving On

Now, do you feel pretty comfortable finding your way around the Expression Web workspace? If so, let's move on to the next step: Creating your first Web site with Expression Web. If you want to take more time and wander around the workspace a bit, that's okay too. Just come on along to Section 3 when you're ready.

3

Creating a Simple Web Site

Expression Web makes it easy for you to start a Web page in whatever way best fits your style. Some people like to begin with a blank page, creating a simple site by adding text, images, links, and other elements that gradually produce the page they're envisioning. Other people dread seeing that blank page—what in the world are you going to put there?—and are relieved when they can begin a new creative effort with helpful hints from a professionally designed template.

Expression Web makes the process simple whether you want to start from scratch or use a template. In fact, Expression Web includes dozens of Dynamic Web Templates, full Web sites that include a header image, main heads, subheads, and text. There are even a few links thrown in. All you need to do is replace the placeholder information with your own content, and you're halfway to a finished Web site! If you'd rather start with a fresh canvas and experiment with styles and placement and images, you can do that easily too.

This section shows you how to start working on that first Web page. Additionally, you'll learn a number of site management techniques, such as opening, importing, renaming, exporting, and deleting sites, and find out how to choose your perspective when you're working with a site in Expression Web.

Where to Begin

Your first choices in Expression Web are important ones. The way in which you start your site will depend on several things: The type of site you want to create (new or existing? customized or from a template?); which standards are important for the site; and what type of style sheet (if any) you will be using to control the format of the text, images, and other elements on your pages.

See Also

To learn more about Dynamic Web Templates, see "Working with Pages" on page 39. In that section, you'll also find resources for information on ASP.NET and Master Pages, which are topics a bit too advanced for the "plain and simple" approach of this book.

Creating a New Site: Your Choices

Choose . . .	When You Want to . . .
One Page Web Site	Create a simple site with a single page (default.htm).
Empty Web Site	Start with a blank site that includes no files and folders so that you can create your own pages from scratch, choose a CSS or frames layout, or add a page based on a Dynamic Web Template or ASP.NET Master Page.
Import Site Wizard	Open, save, and work with an existing Web site in Expression Web.

Creating a One-Page Web Site

Chances are that most of the Web sites you create will be larger than a single page, but a simple one-page site has lots of good uses. You might create a single-page site to be a landing page providing links to other online sources. You might use a one-page site just to let the world know you've got your own virtual space in the online world. Or perhaps this one-pager will simply be the starting point for many pages you add as your site grows.

Start with a One-Page Site

(1) Open the File menu.

(2) Point to New and then click Web Site.

(3) In the New dialog box, on the Web Site tab, click General.

(4) Click One Page Web Site.

(5) If you want to save the site in a folder other than the one displayed in the Specify the Location of the Web Site box at the bottom of the dialog box, click the Browse button to display the New Web Site Location dialog box, choose the folder in which you want to store the site files, and click Open.

(6) Click OK to display the new one-page Web site in the Editing window.

Tip ✓

Expression Web automatically saves the new Web site when you create it; you don't need to do anything special in order to save the site. You will need to save Web pages after you make changes to them, though. Expression Web will prompt you to save any changes on a page before you close an open site, preview the page in your Web browser, or attempt to open a new site.

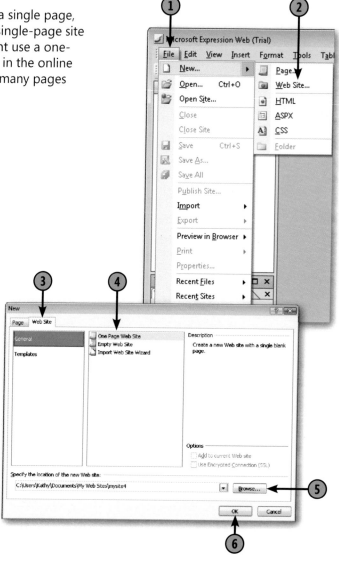

Beginning with an Empty Web Site

Empty Web sites are for those blank-slate people who enjoy the challenge (or freedom, depending on how you look at it) of creating a site completely from scratch. You may want to create an empty site when you plan to add CSS or HTML layouts, create a forms page, add a Dynamic Web Template, or import pages from an existing site.

Create an Empty Web Site

1. Open the File menu.

2. Point to New and then click Web Site.

3. In the New dialog box, on the Web Site tab, click General.

4. Click Empty Web Site.

5. Click Browse if you want to change the folder in which the site will be stored.

6. Click OK to create the site. What you see before you is a totally empty, not-even-a-page-to-look-at site.

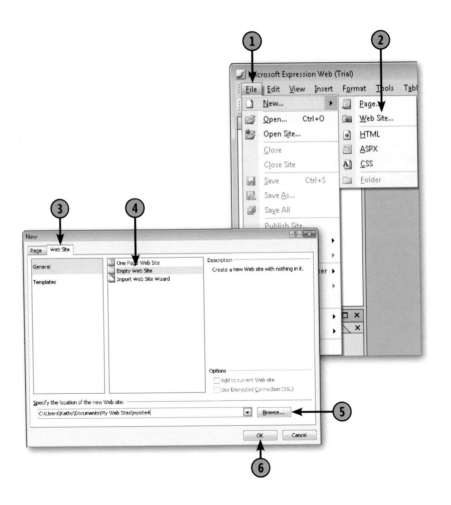

See Also

You'll learn much more about working with Cascading Style Sheets in "Working with Styles and Style Sheets" on page 197.

Importing an Existing Site

Expression Web includes an Import Web Site Wizard that walks you through the process of importing a site (or files you want to use on your site) from a drive, CD, or folder on your local system or from a remote location. Maybe you've previously created and published a simple FrontPage Web site that you want to use in a new site you're creating. Or perhaps someone in your organization sent you a link to a library of files you want to use in the new Web site you're designing with Expression Web. Either way, the Import Web Page Wizard helps you make the connection so you can import your files easily.

Start the Import Process

① Open the File menu.

② Point to New; then click Web Site.

③ In the New dialog box, on the Web Site tab, click Import Web Site Wizard.

④ Click Browse and use the New Web Site Location dialog box to indicate where you want the resulting Web site to be stored.

⑤ Click OK to continue. The Import Web Site Wizard begins and leads you through a series of steps for copying the files to your new site.

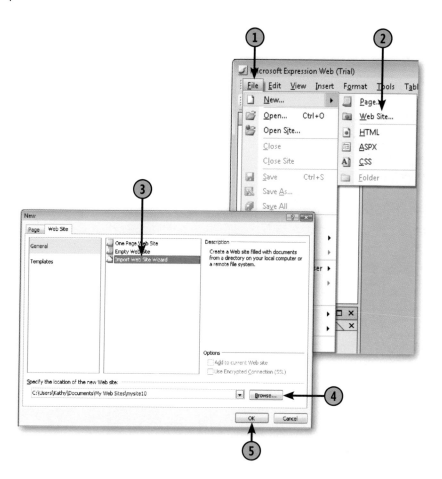

Selecting the Current File Location

1. Select the method you wish to use to access the files.

2. In the Web Site Location box, enter the folder or site URL where the files are currently stored.

3. If you want to include any subsites that are part of the site you're importing, select the Include Subsites check box. (This option is available only for the File System selection.)

4. Click Next to continue.

Choosing Where You Want the Files to Go

1. Type the location for the Web site files and folders. The default path used for your Expression Web site appears in the box.

2. If you want to add the imported files to the Web site you are currently working on, leave the Add to Current Site check box selected, and click Next.

3. Click Finish on the last page of the Wizard.

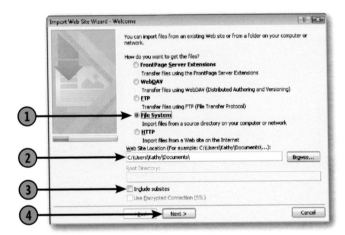

Tip

The most common methods for getting the files are FTP, File System (in which you simply specify the folder on your computer in which the files are stored), and HTTP (which imports files directly from an existing Web site).

Finishing the Import

1 After you click Finish, Remote Web Site view is displayed.

2 In the Local Web Site list, double-click the name of the folder in which you want to save the incoming files.

3 In the Remote Web Site list, select all the files you want to copy.

4 In the Publish all changed pages area, click the item that reflects the way in which you want the pages to be updated. Remote to local tells Expression Web to update the files on the Local Site with any changes found in the files on the Remote Site.

5 Click Publish Web site to complete the process and make the Web site files available in Expression Web.

Try This!

To select all files in the list, click the top item, press and hold the Shift key, and click the bottom item. The entire list is selected.

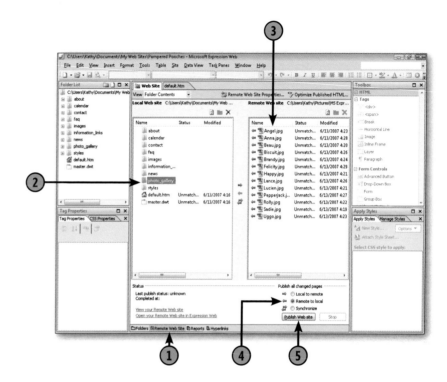

Starting with a Template

If you like the idea of being able to see what others have done with a site before you put your own ideas to work, you'll want to check out Expression Web's templates. You can choose from 19 different templates in three basic styles: Organization, Personal, and Small Business.

Use a Site Template

① Click File and click New; select the Web Site tab.

② Click Templates.

③ Click a template from the displayed list; a preview appears on the right side of the dialog box.

④ When you've found the template you want to use, click OK to create the site.

Try This!

Choose a template to use to begin your Expression Web experience. Open the File menu and click New. Click the Web Site tab and click Templates. Scroll through the list until you find a template style you like; click it. Click OK to open the new site.

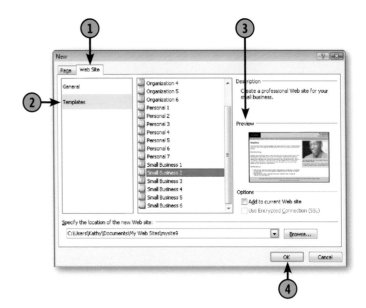

Tip

Best advice before beginning? Know who will be coming to your site. What do they expect to see when they get to your site? What colors, tone, images, and special features will appeal to them? How can you make their lives easier? What do you want them to do when they visit? Answering each of these questions clearly, up-front, will help you ensure that the Web site does what you hope it will do. If you are using a template to get started, knowing what your visitor expects to see helps you choose the right look and feel to begin with.

What's in a Template?

When you create a site based on an Expression Web template, a whole site is created with all the files, folders, links, and placeholder text and images the site involves. As you work with the template files and make them your own, you will

move, rename, edit, and perhaps delete or recreate pages and folders—but when you're just starting out, it's nice to have something to work with.

Web pages in template ──────

Dynamic Web Template ──────

Default home page ──────

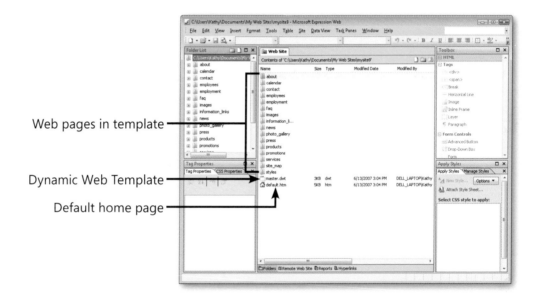

Tip

The file with the extension .dwt is the Dynamic Web Template on which your Expression Web site is based. Dynamic Web Templates include all the elements you'd expect to see in a Web site—headings, text, links, and images. You learn how to work with and customize Dynamic Web Templates in Section 4, "Working with Pages."

Opening an Existing Web Site

Expression Web is friendly with most Web sites you'll try to open; it's a fair assumption to think that if you can open it on the Web, you can open it in Expression Web.

Open a Web Site

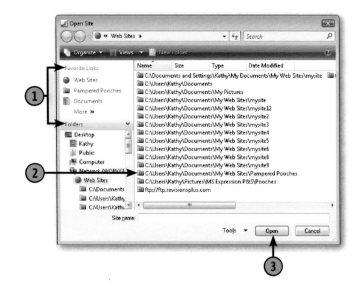

(1) Open the File menu, click Open Site, and navigate to the site by doing one of the following:

- In the top left portion of the Open Site dialog box, click the link where your site is stored in the Favorite Links panel.

- In the lower left portion of the Open Site dialog box, click in the Folders list and navigate to the site you want to open.

(2) Click the icon of the site you want to open.

(3) Click Open.

Try This!

Adding files to an existing site is super easy. Use Windows Explorer to open the folder with the files you want to add to Expression Web. Select the files or folders and drag them to the folder in the Folder List where you want them to be stored. This is a great way to place images, text files, or even style sheets within easy reach while you're working with Expression Web. You can also use this method to easily copy files from one Expression Web site to another.

Tip ✓

Expression Web will automatically display the last Web site you worked on when you start the program (unless you used Close Site before ending your last work session). So if you are working with an existing site and need to wrap up for the afternoon, simply save your file and leave things the way they are, then close Expression Web by choosing Exit in the File menu. When you start Expression Web again, the site will open to the page and view you were using when you ended your last session.

Renaming a Web Site

If you accepted Expression Web's proposed name for your new site when you created it (for example, *mysite4*), one of the first things you may want to do with your new site is give it a new name.

Rename a Web Site

① Click the Site menu.

② Click Site Settings; the General tab of the Site Settings dialog box appears.

③ Type the new name for the site in lowercase letters.

④ Click OK to save the site with the new name.

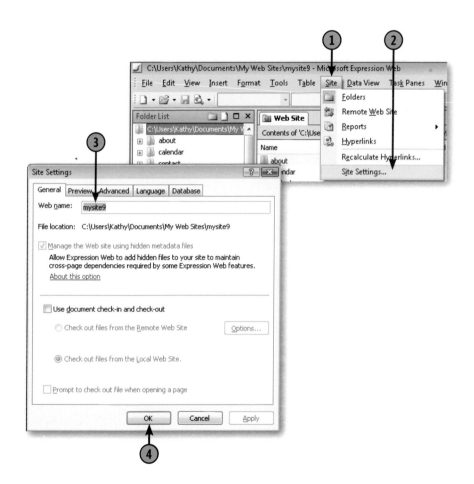

A Little about Renaming

When you first create your Web site in Expression Web, the program supplies a site name for you. Admittedly, it's not very original (*mysite1*, *mysite2*, and so on). But there is rhyme and reason to the naming convention, and there are a few important things you should remember when you go to rename your sites.

Tip ✓

With the exception of the Web Name box in the General tab, the items you'll find in the Site Settings dialog box are beyond what you need to be concerned with when you're learning Expression Web. If you will be working with ASP.NET or creating sophisticated data applications for your Web site, you will use several of the features found in Site Settings.

- Your Web sites are most likely saved by default in a folder that looks like this: c:\My Documents\My Web Sites\mysite. You can change the folder or create subfolders if you like, but it's a good idea to keep your sites in the My Web Sites folder. This not only makes it easier for you to find what you're looking for, but also enables you to back up the entire folder for safekeeping.

- The standard convention of naming files is all lowercase, and because the code on your pages is case-sensitive, it's a good idea to stick with that plan. Name your sites using only lowercase letters to sidestep any file problems later in your site design and publishing.

- Because a Web site is actually a collection of a number of files and folders (take a look at your Folders List in the Expression Web window if you're wondering about this), when you rename a site, you are impacting a number of items within those files and folders.

- Choose a distinctive name that will help you remember the content of the file. Better yet, come up with a consistent naming plan for all the sites you create. Right now, when you're just starting, you may think you'll recall a site named *newsite*, but after designing 10 or 15 sites, you won't be able to remember what's in it without opening it.

Exporting a Web Site

At some point in your life as a Web designer, it's likely that you'll want to export files from one Web site to be used in another. Perhaps you really like the way you did the About Us page on a particular site and you'd like to use it in other sites as well. Exporting a file leaves the original file in place and exports a copy of it to a new location you specify.

Export a File from Your Site

1. In the Folder List or Web Site view, click the file you want to export.

2. Open the File menu.

3. Point to Export and then click File.

4. In the Export Selected As dialog box, choose the folder to which you want to export the file.

5. Click the Save As Type arrow and choose the format for the exported file.

6. Enter a new name, if you like, in the File Name box.

7. Click Save to export the file.

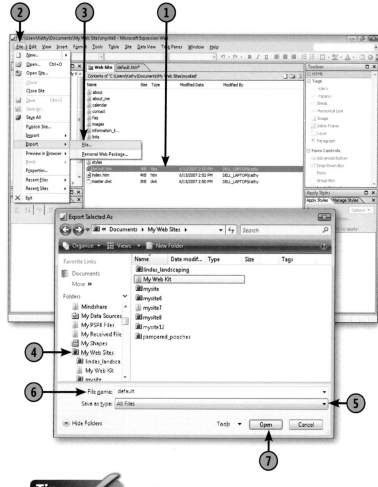

Export Possibilities: Save As Type Options

Save in This Format . . .	When You Want To . . .
HTML	Use the file as a page in another Web site.
GIF and JPEG	Use the file as an image in another Web site or document.
Microsoft Office Files	Work with the file in a Microsoft Office application.

Tip

When you export a file, only the selected file is exported to the new location. If the file relies on other files (such as images or a style sheet), you will also need to export those files to the new location in order for the page to display properly.

Expression Web gives you the option of creating a Personal Web Package for those times when you want to put together a group of files that you can export and use in other sites and applications. Begin by opening the site containing the files and folders you want to include in the personal Web package. Open the File menu, point to Export, and click Personal Web Package. In the

Export Web Package dialog box, choose the files and folders you want to include; then click Add to add them to the Web package. If you want to view all the files and folders your selected items need to display and function properly (these are known as dependencies), click the Show Dependencies button. Click OK to create the personal Web package.

Deleting a Web Site

At some point you will need to delete a Web site you've created. Perhaps you started one and got a better idea. Maybe you were just experimenting with Expression Web features. Whatever the reason for the discard, it's time to remove those unneeded sites.

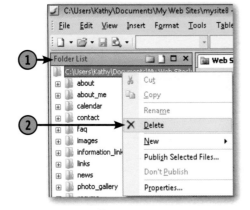

① In the Folder List, right-click the Web site you want to delete.

② Click Delete.

③ In the Confirm Delete dialog box, specify whether you want to delete only the hidden information about the site and keep the files and folders (which you might want to do when you are preparing the site to pass on to another person to work with) or delete the entire site.

④ Click OK to finish the process.

Tip

Both Windows Vista and Windows XP enable you to rename and delete files directly in the Open and Save As dialog boxes as well as in Windows Explorer. If you rename or delete files in this way, however, the changes will not be reflected in Expression Web. When you navigate to a folder containing a file you renamed, for example, the new name may not appear, because Expression Web remembers files you selected previously. If you double-click the old name of the file to open it, Expression Web will display an error, saying that the file cannot be found. For best results, delete and rename files directly in Expression Web so the program knows what's going on (which saves time and trouble for you).

Viewing Site Information

Now that you've worked a bit with files, folders, and sites, you have no doubt noticed that there are several ways to view your site in Expression Web. The View buttons appear along the bottom edge of the Editing window. You can move from one view to another easily by clicking the button of the view you want to see. Or, if you prefer, you can open the Site menu to display view choices and make your selection there.

Click a view button to change the display in the Editing window

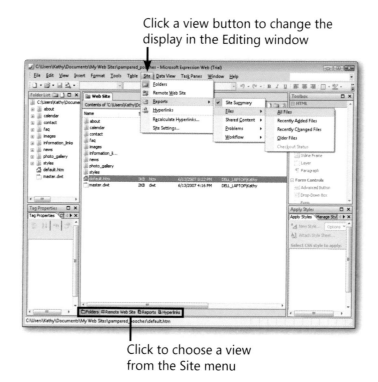

Click to choose a view from the Site menu

Getting Perspective with Site Views

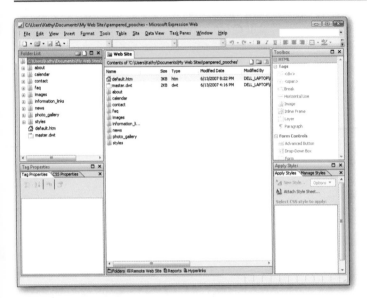

Folders view is the view that is displayed when you first begin working with Expression Web. Here you see all the files and folders in your site. You can move from one page to another by clicking the item in the list you want to display.

Remote Web Site view shows you both the files and folders on your local computer and the files and folders on a site you are connected to on the server where you are publishing your site. You can use Remote Web Site to publish a new site or update an existing one.

(continued on the next page)

Tip

Confused about views? The views introduced here are all site views—in other words, they give you different perspectives of the overall site. When you are working with a specific page, another set of view options enables you to work with the page in different ways: Design view shows you the layout of the page, Split view displays both the layout and the code behind the layout, and Code view shows you the code only.

Getting Perspective with Site Views *(continued)*

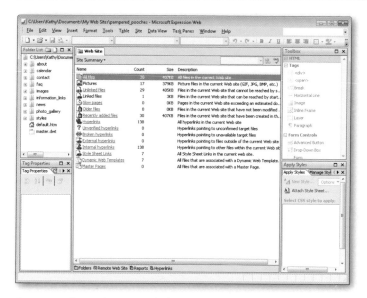

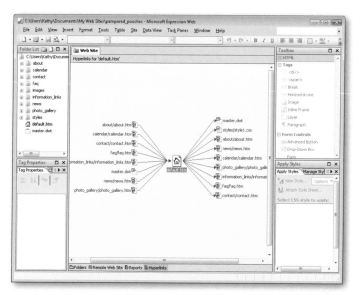

Reports view gives you information about your site and enables you to produce more detailed site reports.

Hyperlinks view displays a diagram of all the links that take users to a specific file or, alternately, a diagram of all links from a specific file.

Try This!

With the new template-based site you created open in the workspace, click Site and point to Reports. Now point to Shared Content, and click Dynamic Web Templates. A report appears in Reports view, listing a number of Web pages (with the .htm extension). The file master.dwt (the master template for the site) is also included in the list. This report lists the files that share content with the template you used to create the site and provides the file name, location, and folder name of each of the files.

Moving On

Congratulations! You created your first Web site in Expression Web and learned all the basic site management techniques you'll need as you design and share sites from now on. That's a big chunk of the necessary work. In the next section, you move in closer to learn how to work with your site's pages and begin splashing some creativity on the page by creating a page background, tweaking templates, and more.

Working with Pages

4

Once you create a Web site, you're ready to add and work with pages. The Web page is where all the action happens on your site. Each Web page is stored as a separate file and can include images, text, headings, links, and sound and video objects.

Depending on whether you created your site with a blank Web page or based it on a Dynamic Web Template, you may or may not already have Web pages in your site. If you created your site from scratch, you will use the techniques in this section to add, open, close, rename, save, and apply master formatting to the pages in your site. If you used a Dynamic Web Template, Web pages are already included for you, so the techniques most helpful to you in this chapter will likely be the ones that enable you to open, rename, save, and delete the existing pages in the template.

Creating a New Page

Now that you know how to create a new Web site, you're ready to begin adding pages. Of course, if you created the Web site by using one of Expression Web's templates, you've already got default pages to work with. The process of adding a new page to the site is as simple as clicking a button on the Common toolbar.

Add a New Page

① In the Common toolbar, click the New Document arrow

② Click HTML. The blank page appears in the Editing window with a generated name such as Untitled_1.htm displayed in the page tab.

New Page Choices in Expression Web

Page Type	Purpose
HTML	Creates a standard HTML Web page so that you can add text, images, links, and more.
ASPX	Creates a page you can use with Expression Web master pages and ASP.NET controls.
CSS	Opens a blank document so that you can create a Cascading Style Sheet.

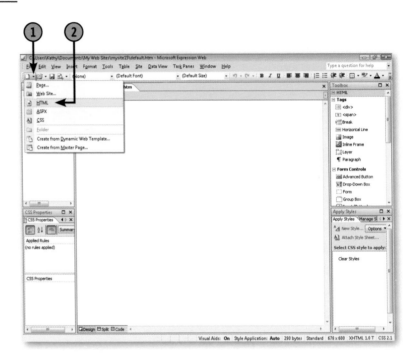

Tip

You can also open the File menu and click New to start a new page. Click HTML and then click OK, to create your Web page.

Create a New Page Based on an Existing Page

1 In the Folder List, right-click the existing page you want to use.

2 Click New From Existing Page.

Add Pages in the Folder List

1 Open the Web site you want to add pages to.

2 In the Folder List, right-click the folder in which you want to add the new page.

3 Point to New.

4 Click HTML.

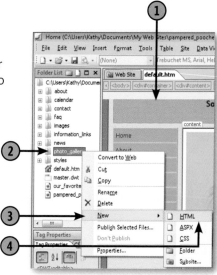

Adding the Master Design

When you add a page by choosing New Document (or by pressing Ctrl+N), a blank page appears in the Editing window. If you're working with a Dynamic Web Template, which already includes the page design, navigation bar, and header, you may be wondering how to add those design features to your new blank-at-the-moment page.

Add the Master Design to the New Page

1. Click the Untitled_1.htm tab to select the new page.

2. In the Folder List, click and drag master.dwt to the Editing window.

3. Click Close.

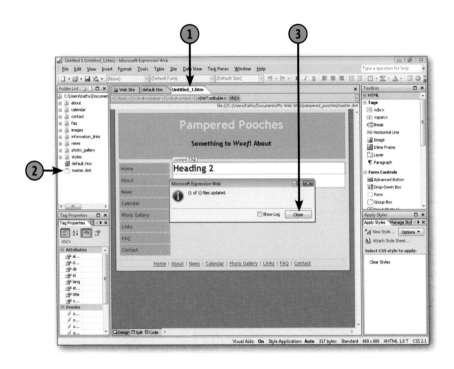

Tip

Wondering what master.dwt stands for? The first part of the file name, master, lets you know that this is the file that contains the design used in all pages of the template. The file extension, .dwt, is short for Dynamic Web Template.

See Also

For more information on Dynamic Web Templates, see "Working with Dynamic Web Templates" on page 51.

Saving the Page

Although Expression Web initially saved your Web site when you created it and will prompt you to save any changes before you close the file, it's always a good idea to take that extra step and save your work each time you add something significant to your site. Saving your file takes only a moment, but it will be a really important moment if you experience a sudden power outage (or your laptop battery dies without warning) and you wind up redoing an afternoon's work.

Save the Page

1. Open the File menu.

2. Click Save As. The Save As dialog box opens.

3. Type a name for the file.

4. Click Change Title. The Set Page Title dialog box appears.

5. Type a title for the page, and then click OK. This is the title that will appear in the browser window when visitors view this page on the Web.

6. Click Save, to save your page.

Try This!

Want a fast save? Press Ctrl+S or click the Save button on the Common toolbar.

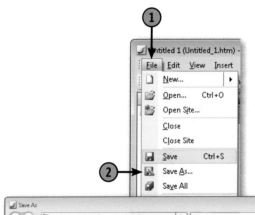

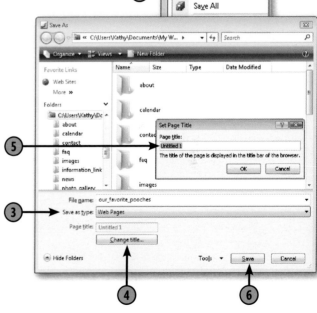

Tip

For best results, be as clear as possible when naming your page. The title of the page is displayed in the Web browser and displayed in search results users view online. If the name of your page isn't easy to understand in a list of search results, potential visitors might click away and go to someone else's site.

Setting Page Properties

Expression Web gives you the option of setting Web page properties to include many specialized features—for example, you can add a customized page background, control the page languages, and make choices about HTML encoding. Three simple but important settings you can add when you first create a new page are the Title, Description, and Keyword settings, all available on the General tab of the Page Properties dialog box.

Add Page Properties

① Right-click anywhere on the new page.

② Click Page Properties.

(continued on the next page)

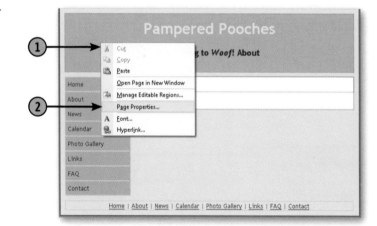

Try This!

Double-click a Web page in the Folder List to open it in the Editing window. Right-click anywhere on the page, and click Page Properties. In the General tab of the Page Properties dialog box, click in the Keywords box and type words and phrases that describe the page.

Add Page Properties *(continued)*

(3) Click in the Title box and type the page title you want to appear in the browser window.

(4) Click in the Page Description box and type a brief description of the page. This description will appear in search results, so try to use strong, interesting words that accurately reflect the page's content.

(5) Click in the Keywords box and enter words and phrases related to the page.

(6) Click OK.

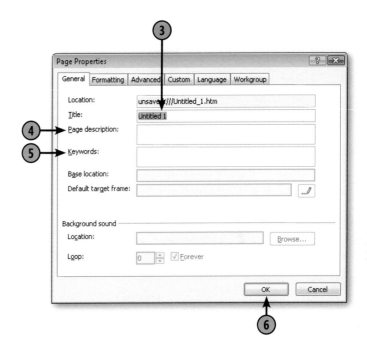

Tip

Keywords are a really important part of making sure your site gets noticed by search engines. Choose words that are likely to be searched for by people you want to come to your site. For example, Pampered Pooches might use pets, dogs, puppies, dog grooming, dog sitting, dog spa, and doggie day care as the keywords for the Our Services page.

Opening a Web Page

Expression Web can open virtually any page you can display on the Web. You have the choice of opening either a full Web site or an additional Web page. Expression Web enables you to have multiple pages open in the Editing window at any one time. You can move among open pages by clicking the tabs at the top of the Editing window.

Open a Web Page

1. On the Common Toolbar click the Open arrow, and then click Open.

2. In the Open File dialog box, navigate to the folder containing the page you want to open.

3. Click the page in the file and folder list.

4. Click Open.

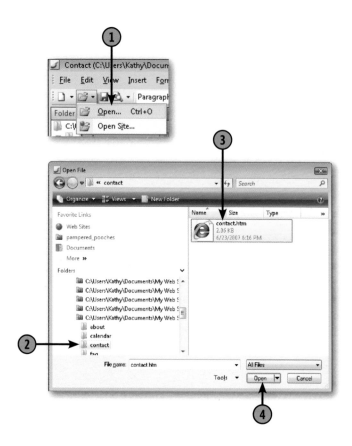

Tip

If you have a site open and displayed in the Folder List, you can open a Web page easily by finding the page in the Folder List and double-clicking it.

Tip

In addition to opening Web pages, you can open just about any other type of file in Expression Web. If you want to view a Microsoft Word document, for example, you can click the Open command on the Common toolbar and navigate to the file you want to open. Double-click the file and Expression Web will launch the application (in this case, Microsoft Word) and display the file.

Closing a Web Page

Closing a Web page is a simple matter of point and click. You can close the page one of two ways: You can open the File menu and click Close, or right-click the page tab in the Editing window and click Close. If you have made changes to the Web page that have not been saved, Expression Web will prompt you to save the changes before you close the page.

Right-click the tab

Click Close

Renaming a Web Page

At various times during your project you may need to rename some or all of the pages in your site. A great feature of Expression Web is the program's ability to update related pages when you make changes to the existing one. When you rename Web pages, Expression Web makes corresponding changes in related files. It's important that you do the renaming within Expression Web, however; if you rename the files using Windows, Expression Web may not know about the page changes, which may result in errors.

Rename a Web Page

① In the Folder List, right-click the page you want to rename.

② Click Rename.

③ Type the new name for the file and then press Enter.

(continued on the next page)

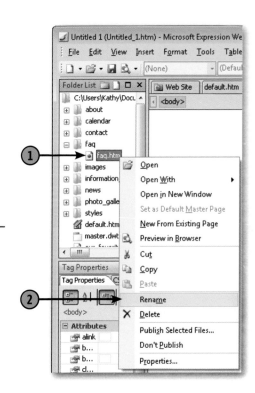

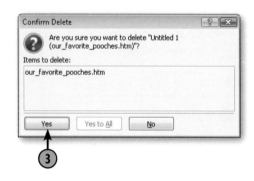

Tip ✓

When you are naming your Web pages, keeping a few rules of thumb in mind can help you cut down on possible page errors. First, use all lowercase letters and choose a name that relates to the page so you'll be able to remember the content later. Next, use underscore characters (_) instead of space. Finally, avoid using any characters that aren't letters or numbers.

Tip ✓

When you are naming your Web pages, keeping a few rules of thumb in mind can help you cut down on possible page errors. First, use all lowercase letters and choose a name that relates to the page so you'll be able to remember the content later. Next, use underscore characters (_) instead of space. Finally, avoid using any characters that aren't letters or numbers.

Tip ✓

When you rename a Web page, be sure to add the .htm at the end of the page name. Otherwise Expression Web won't recognize the page as a Web page.

Deleting a Web Page

As you are learning Expression Web, it's a fair guess that you'll want to discard many pages as you learn new features and try new techniques. Deleting a Web page is a simple matter, and, true to form, Expression Web gives you several ways to do it.

Delete a Web Page

① Open the folder that contains the page you want to delete, and right-click the page.

② Click Delete.

③ In the Confirm Delete dialog box, click Yes.

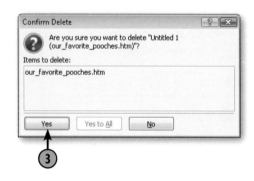

Tip ✓

Undo does not work when it comes to deleting pages; be sure you want to remove a page permanently before you confirm the deletion.

Adding a Page Background

When you are first starting out with Expression Web, you may not want to venture into designing your own page backgrounds. But it is an easier task than you might think. You can easily add a picture to the page background to give the pages of your site a special look.

Add a Page Background

(1) Open the Format menu.

(2) Click Background.

(3) In the Page Properties dialog box, select the Background Picture check box.

(4) Click Browse.

(5) In the Select Background Picture dialog box, select the folder containing the image you want to use.

(6) Click the image.

(7) Click Open.

(8) In the Page Properties dialog box, click OK.

Tip

Page background options aren't available to you if you are working with a site based on a Dynamic Web Template. The master. dwt file contains the information used to create the page background. To add a page with your own custom page background, click New in the Common toolbar and click HTML. A blank page opens, and you can create your own page background.

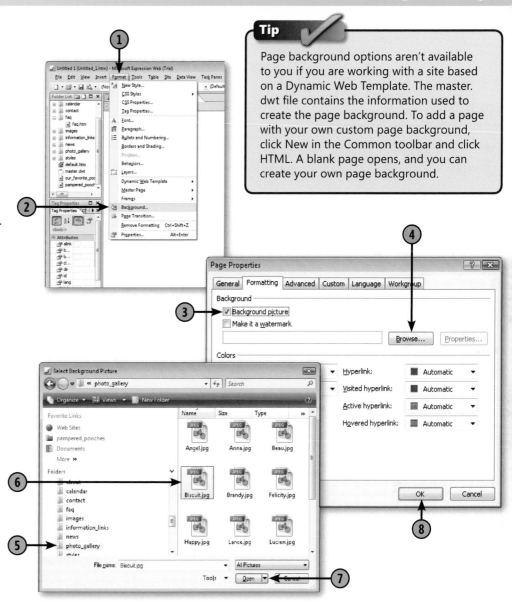

Previewing Web Pages

When you are viewing pages in the Editing window, Design view shows you by default a display similar to the way the page will look on screen. This display is only similar and not exact because of the visual aids Expression Web adds to help you see the elements on the page. To see the way the page will look in a browser window, you need to preview the page.

Preview the Web Page

① In the Common toolbar, click the Preview arrow.

② Click the browser you want to use to view the page.

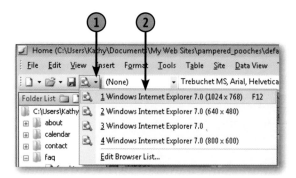

It is a good idea to view your page in different screen resolutions, using different browsers. Because some browsers have different rendering engines (meaning they read and display page elements slightly differently), previewing in multiple browsers helps you anticipate any display problems that might pop up.

Wondering what screen resolution has to do with anything? Displaying the page in other resolutions may result in subtle but important different in your page. Notice the small Page Size resolution setting in the right corner of the Expression Web status bar. The current setting shows the resolution in use (for example, 619 x 584). To display a list of page size settings and choose a different resolution, double-click the Page Size setting in the status bar.

Working with Dynamic Web Templates

In the last section, you learned how easy it is to start a Web site based on a Dynamic Web Template. These templates in Expression Web are HTML-based templates that enable you to apply a ready-made format to pages you specify. Here are some quick facts about Dynamic Web Templates:

- Dynamic Web Templates enable you to apply a format easily to multiple pages.

- You can also use multiple Dynamic Web Templates in a single file.

- Whenever you modify the Dynamic Web Template, the pages based on it change automatically.

- You can detach and attach Dynamic Web Templates at anytime.

- You can use the Dynamic Web Templates as they are provided in Expression Web or modify them as needed.

- You can add editable regions to allow for text and picture changes on each page. Others with the appropriate permissions will be able to edit the content of the sections on those pages.

Tip

An editable region is the area on a Web page that can be edited by others who have the appropriate permissions to add to, modify, or remove content on the Web page. Editable content can be text, images, or links on the page.

Tip

You can also create your own Dynamic Web Template based on an HTML file you already have. You might want to do this, for example, if you have an existing Web page design you want to use as a template for pages you create in Expression Web. Simply open the file in Expression Web (open the File menu and click Open). When the page is open on the screen, open the File menu, click Save As, and select Dynamic Web Template in the Save As Type list. Click Save to save the file as a Dynamic Web Template.

Create a New Dynamic Web Template

1. Open the File menu.
2. Point to New and then click Page.

(continued on the next page)

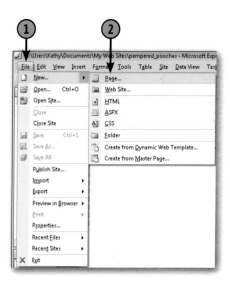

Create a New Dynamic Web Template (continued)

③ Click General.

④ Click Dynamic Web Template.

⑤ Click OK. The Dynamic Web Template page appears in the Editing window in Design view.

Add an Editable Region to a Web Page

① Right-click in the blank area of the new Dynamic Web Template.

② Click Manage Editable Regions.

(continued on the next page)

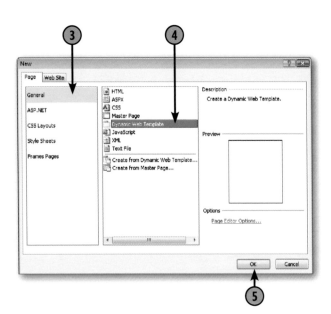

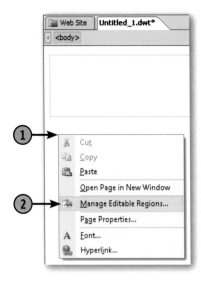

Tip ✓

Display the Dynamic Web Template toolbar by opening the View menu, pointing to Toolbars, and then clicking Dynamic Web Template. You can use the Dynamic Web Template Toolbar to work with editable regions on your pages, update pages to reflect template changes, and attach new templates.

Tip ✓

Be sure that you click a blank area of the page if you want to add an editable region. If you select Manage Editable Regions when an editable region of the page is selected, the Add command will not be available.

Add an Editable Region to a Web Page *(continued)*

③ Type a name for the region.

④ Click Add.

⑤ Click Close.

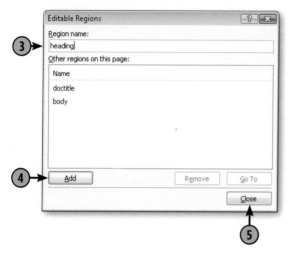

③ ④ ⑤

Tip

You can add as many regions as you like on a Dynamic Web Template. Simply click in a new area of the page and add a new region by repeating these steps.

Tip

Resizing an editable region is easy. Simply click the region on the page and drag one of the handles in the direction you want to resize the region.

Attach a Web Template to a Page

① Open the Web page to which you want to attach the Dynamic Web Template.

② Open the Format menu.

③ Point to Dynamic Web Template and click Attach Dynamic Web Template.

(continued on the next page)

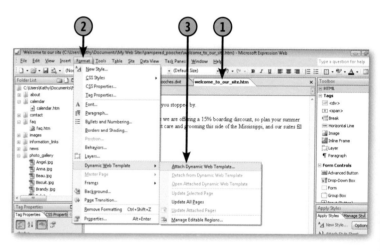

Tip

If the editable regions you've created on the Dynamic Web Template do not match exactly the regions on the Web page you're applying the template to, the Match Editable Regions dialog box will appear. Click the content items in the list that need to be resolved; then click OK to accept the template regions. Alternately, you can click the item and click Modify to tell Expression Web from which region on the new page should be assigned to the editable regions in the template.

④ Click the folder containing the template you want to use.

⑤ Select the template file in the file and folder list.

⑥ Click Open.

Tip

The process of detaching a Dynamic Web Template is just as easy as attaching one. Display the page to which the template has been applied; then open the Format menu, click Dynamic Web Template, and click Detach From Dynamic Web Template. The content of the page remains, but any further updates to the Dynamic Web Template will not be reflected in the page.

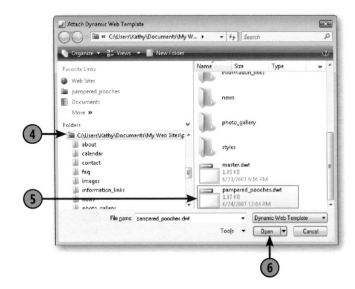

Moving On

In this section, you learned a variety of page creation and management techniques. Now you know how to add pages, as well as open, close, delete, save, and apply templates to them.

The next section kicks into creative high gear by giving you the opportunity to practice writing and formatting content as you add text to your Web pages.

Adding and Editing Text

This is where it really gets interesting. You've created your Web site and now know how to add pages. Whether you started your site with a Dynamic Web Template (which means you already have pages and sample text in your site) or you began with a blank page, it's time to turn your story into words on the page.

This section focuses on your text in two different ways. First, you'll learn how to add the content—by typing directly onto the page, importing text, or copying and pasting text from another page or application. Then you'll format the text so that it appears on the page just the way you want it to, with attractive headings, easy-to-read bullets, numbered lists, and more.

Entering Text

Expression Web makes it easy for you to get text on the page, whether you're typing it from scratch, copying and pasting it from another application, or borrowing it from another Web page you've already created (and perfected!).

Replace Template Text

Tip

Of course, you don't need to type the text to replace the text that's already there. If you're copying a paragraph from another document, just select the text you want to replace and paste the new text in the same space. The text is automatically replaced with the new content.

1. Open the Web site you want to work with.

2. In the Folder List, double-click the page with the content you want to replace.

3. Highlight the placeholder text and type the text to replace it.

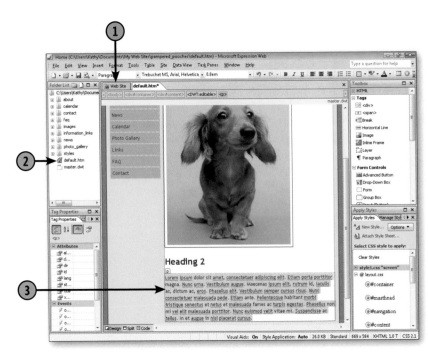

Add Text

1. Open the page on which you want to enter text.

2. Click on the page and start typing.

3. Press Enter. Expression Web creates a new paragraph.

Tip

Spend some time browsing before you begin writing your own text. Which text styles do you like on other peoples' sites—casual and friendly? Professional and authoritative? Add the sites you like to your Favorites so that you can refer back to them as you create the text for your own site.

Tip

Yes, we know there's a little typo in that last paragraph. You'll find out how to fix that in "Correcting Spelling," later in this section.

Drag and Drop Text

1 Open the document with the text you want to drag and drop.

2 Select the text.

3 Click and drag the mouse pointer from the selected text to the place on your Web page you want the text to appear; release the mouse button.

Tip

Expression Web works great with all Microsoft Office applications (including Word 2007, shown here). Basically any information you can copy and paste on the Clipboard can be used in Expression Web—which may save you a lot of typing! Read on to find out more about copying and pasting information on your pages.

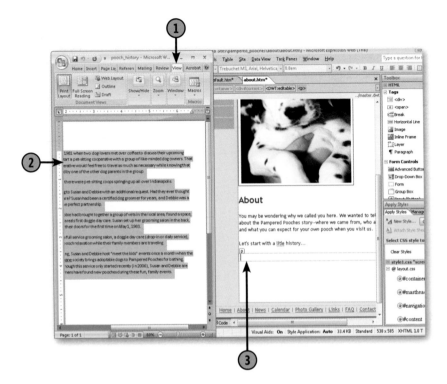

Copying and Pasting Text

Your basic copy-and-paste procedure is a common part of every computer program known to humankind, and it's easy to understand why. This simple operation keeps you from having to redo what you've already done, recreate the wheel,

or, at least, retype text you've already entered once. Expression Web is very flexible with the pasting part, too, giving you choices for controlling whether the pasted text brings its previous format and spacing into your current page.

Copy Text

(1) Open the Web site that contains the text you want to copy.

(2) In the Folder List, double-click the page you want to display.

(3) Highlight the text.

(4) Right-click the highlighted text and choose Copy.

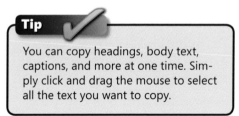

Tip ✓

You can copy headings, body text, captions, and more at one time. Simply click and drag the mouse to select all the text you want to copy.

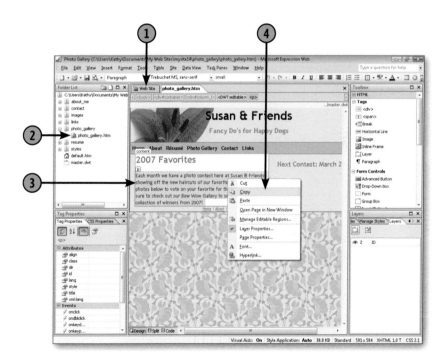

Paste Text

① Open the Web site where you want to paste the text.

② In the Folder List, double-click the page you want to display.

③ Highlight any text you want to replace, or click on the page to create a new paragraph.

④ Right-click and choose Paste. Immediately after you paste the text, a small paste button appears beside the paragraph, offering four different formatting options for the pasted text.

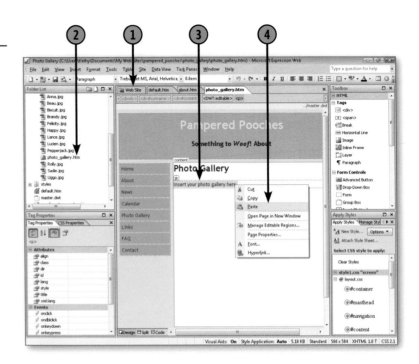

Tip ✓

Are you wondering whether you really have to deal with all these paste choices? For most traditional paste jobs, you don't need to worry about formats, line spacing, and such. But if you paste text into your page and it doesn't look right or does something unexpected, press Ctrl+Z to undo the paste and then consider using one of the paste options to see whether it turns out better the second time.

Tip ✓

The Paste Text command in the Edit menu provides you with additional paste options that enable you to paste plain text, single or multiple pre-formatted paragraphs, or for-matted paragraphs with or without line breaks. To display the Paste Text dialog box, open the Edit menu, and click Paste Text.

Understanding Paste Options

Use This	To Do This
Keep Source Formatting	Retain the same formatting applied to the source of the copied text.
Remove Formatting	Remove the formatting used in the source text so the text appears as plain text.
Keep HTML Only	Keep the rendered HTML of pasted text (for example, \boldface\ appears as **boldface**).
Keep Text Only	Paste the text as straight text with no formatting.

Simple Formatting

Straight text on a bare page isn't going to hold anyone's interest very long on today's Web. There is just too much competition offering color, flashy fonts and streaming, beeping, blinking media. The format of your text adds a little (not too much!) visual excitement to your page. A good format also shows you know what you're doing, so it's worth a little investment.

Tip

Here are a couple of quick text selection tricks. To select a word, simply click to position the mouse pointer anywhere in it. To select a paragraph, press and hold Alt while clicking in the paragraph.

Make Text Bold

① Display the page you want to change.

② Select the text.

③ In the Common toolbar, click Bold.

Add Italics to Text

① Display the page you want to change.

② Select the text.

③ Click Italic in the Common toolbar.

Code assigned to selected text

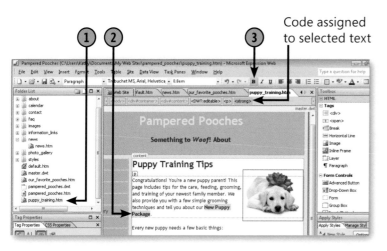

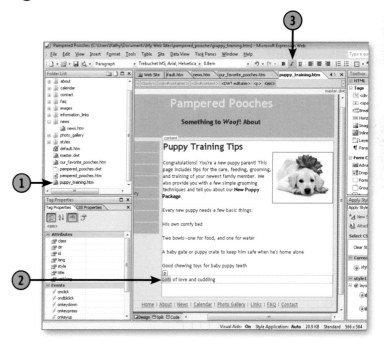

Tip

Looking for a quick bold technique? Use Ctrl+B.

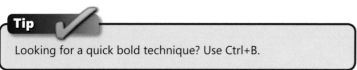

Choose Text Alignment

① Display the page with the content you want to change.

② Select the text.

③ Click one of the following tools in the Common toolbar:

 **Align Text Left**

 Center

Align Text Right

Tip

Expression Web automatically assumes you want text to be aligned left at the start; so at first the Align Text Left button won't appear to do anything. After you click Center or Align Text Right, however, you'll be able to return the text to left alignment by clicking Align Text Left.

Tip

Different is good, but don't go too far in trying to make your Web page stand out by shaking up the format of your text. Centering long passages of text on your page will only annoy your readers (it makes them work too hard to understand what you're trying to say). When it comes to things as basic as text alignment, sticking pretty close to convention (left alignment) is the safest way to meet your readers' expectations--except for those times you really have something special and want to call attention to it.

Working with Fonts

The word *font* refers to the look of the text in your document or on your Web page. A *font* is one size and style of a set of characters in a particular typeface family. The fonts you use on your Web page are important because each different typeface conveys a different tone. Some are professional and no-non-sense (like Times New Roman). Others are more casual, providing the information you need (such as Arial). And still others are playful and fun, saying, in effect, "Don't take me too seriously" (like Comic Sans).

A Few Font Guidelines

Easy does it	Resist the temptation to go hog wild with fonts. One font for the body content and one for headings will keep things simple and readable for your site visitors.
Say it, don't shout it	NEVER USE CAPITALS!!! (or multiple exclamation points). Your readers will think you are being overly dramatic and click away from your site (and miss your point completely).
Play nice with others	Remember that not everyone will be viewing your pages with the same type of computer hardware and software you use. Keep your fonts simple—limiting them to the most common ones on the Web (or create a font family, as you learn to do later in this section).
Size does matter	People have different preferences for the size of the text they like to read online. Most news sites use a fairly small font (like 8.5-point Verdana), perhaps to get as much information as possible on the page; some instructional sites use huge fonts (such as 14-point Arial). Most of us are comfortable somewhere in between.

Make Major Font Changes—Fast

1. In the Folder List, double-click the page you want to use.

2. Select the text.

3. Open the Format menu.

4. Click Font.

(continued on the next page)

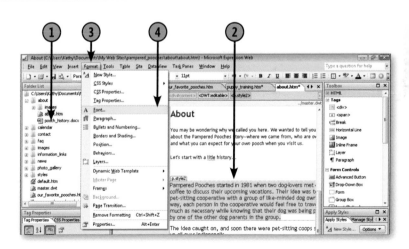

Click to choose a style

5 Select your choices in the Font dialog box and click OK to save the changes.

Scroll through the list and click the font you want

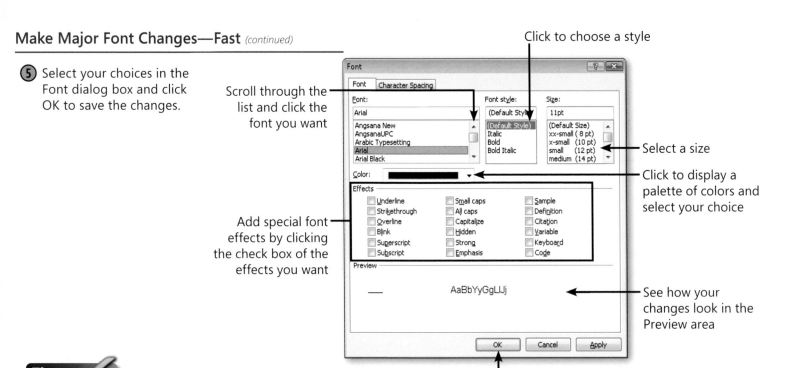

Select a size

Click to display a palette of colors and select your choice

Add special font effects by clicking the check box of the effects you want

See how your changes look in the Preview area

Tip ✓

Points and pixels, pixels and points. Let's clear up any jargon confusion that may be floating around in the back of your head. A point is a typographical term used to refer to the size of a particular font. One point is 1/72 of an inch, so if you want your heading to appear in one-inch characters, you would choose a 72-point font. Pixels, on the other hand, is the measurement term used to refer to items that are displayed on the screen. Typically type is not measured in pixels, although you will see some mixing of the two in Expression Web. You choose the Font Size (in points) in the Font dialog box and using the Font Size tool in the Common toolbar, but you specify the spacing you want to appear between characters (in the Character Spacing tab of the Font dialog box), by entering the spacing value in pixels.

Tip ✓

If you want to make multiple changes in the Font dialog box, you can see how the changes look on your page while you continue to make changes. Simply click Apply to apply the font changes to the selected text on your page. You can then continue to make changes in the Font dialog box or click OK to save what you've done.

Change Font Type from the Common Toolbar

1. In the Folder List, double-click the page that contains the text you want to change.
2. Highlight the text.
3. Click the Font arrow in the Common toolbar.
4. Click the Font you want to apply to the selected text.

Select Font Size

1. In the Folder List, double-click the page you want to change.
2. Select the text.
3. Click the Font Size arrow and click the font size you want to apply.

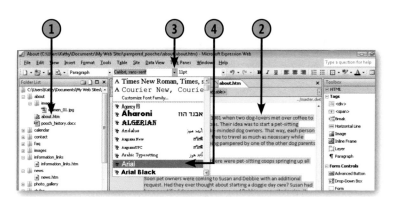

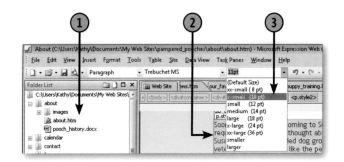

See Also

Are you wondering where styles enter in to all of this? Styles are a type of preset format that you apply to your text (and other elements on your page) that take care of things like font selection, size, color, and style. You'll find out how to use Expression Web's ready-made styles in "Applying Styles," later in this section. And for the play-by-play on attaching CSS style sheets and creating and using CSS styles on your Web pages, see "Working with Styles and Style Sheets" on page 197.

Tip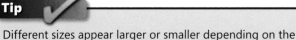

Different sizes appear larger or smaller depending on the font you have selected. For example, 10-point Verdana looks a lot bigger and blockier than 10-point Times New Roman. Experiment with fonts to get the sizing and effect you like, but remember that 10-point type may mean different effects in different font families.

Change Font Color

1. In the Folder List, double-click the page you want to work with.

2. Select the text.

3. Click the Font Color arrow and click a color from the displayed palette.

Click to choose a standard Web color

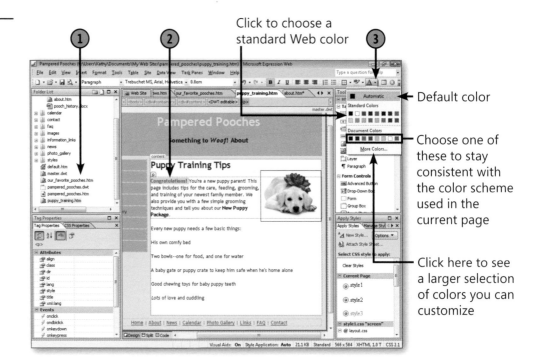

Default color

Choose one of these to stay consistent with the color scheme used in the current page

Click here to see a larger selection of colors you can customize

Creating a New Font Family

Not all fonts look good on the Web, and some browsers do a better job of displaying fonts than others. If a user's browser doesn't have the specific font you've used on your Web page, the font substituted on the user's system may not look nearly as nice as the one you selected. You can get around this by creating a font family, which gives browsers a range of choices for the fonts they display. This enables you to give the browser a range of choices so that if the first choice doesn't work, the browser will automatically go to the second font in the list.

Create a Font Family

① Click the Font arrow on the Common toolbar.

② Click Customize Font Family.

③ Click (New Font Family).

④ In the Add font list, click the first font you want to include in the family.

⑤ Click Add. Repeat to add additional fonts.

⑥ Click OK to save the font family.

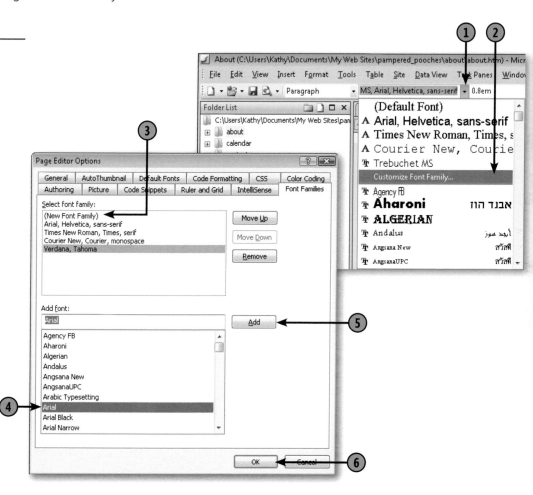

To Serif or Not to Serif

In the Select Font Family list, three families appear by default. The first is a sans-serif family and it includes Arial and Helvetica. The second is a serif family, including Times New Roman and Times. The third is a monospace family, and it includes Courier New and Courier. The terms *serif, sans-serif,* and *monospace* each refer to the way in which the characters are formed. Here's how each one differs:

In a serif font, the characters have small lines at the ends of the strokes in the letter. A sans-serif font (which means, literally, "without serif") has no extenders on the characters—it provides a cleaner, less formal look. A monospace font is one in which each character is given exactly the same space as every other character (which isn't true for either serif or sans-serif fonts). You can see the differences easily here:

> Expression Web - serif
>
> **Expression Web - sans-serif**
>
> `Expression Web - monospace`

The type of fonts you choose and the font families you create depend on the tone and feel you want for your site as well as your own personal preference. Take a look around the Web and find out what designers are using on other Web sites you like to read. The key is readability—if the font you choose helps people enjoy their time on your site, they are likely to come back (and bring friends!).

Controlling the Spacing of Your Text

Spacing is one of those tricky areas that many new designers struggle with when they are just starting out. You always seem to have too much space between paragraphs—or not enough. Or your text runs right up to the edge of the page—or stops too short. This section gives you a few simple techniques for making sure your spacing is just the way you want it.

Set Paragraph Spacing

① In the Folder List, double-click the page you want to work with.

② Open the Format menu.

③ Click Paragraph.

(continued on the next page)

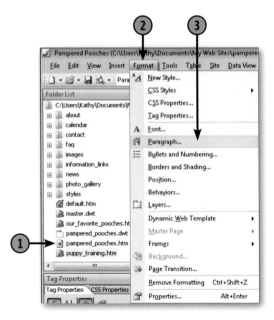

Set Paragraph Spacing *(continued)*

④ Enter your settings and click OK to save the changes.

Tip ✓

You can also control the spacing between characters in your text by using the Character Spacing tab in the Font dialog box. Display the dialog box by clicking Font from the Format menu. Then click Character Spacing, and click the Spacing arrow. Choose either Expanded or Condensed and enter a spacing value (in points) in the By box. Click OK to save the spacing settings.

Controls the amount of space on the right and left edges of text paragraphs

Controls spacing between paragraphs

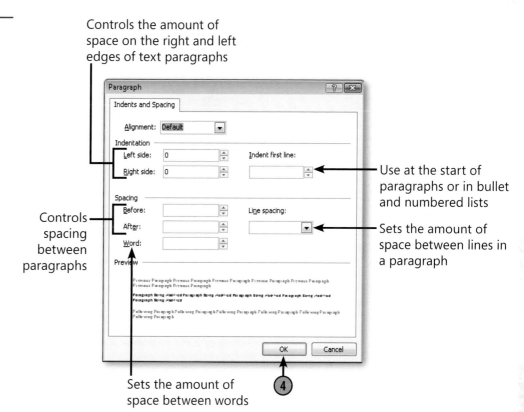

Use at the start of paragraphs or in bullet and numbered lists

Sets the amount of space between lines in a paragraph

Sets the amount of space between words

Using the Format Painter

If you're familiar with other Microsoft programs, you've probably met the Format Painter, a tool that enables you to pick up a format you've already used and "paint" it onto other areas of your document. The Format Painter can be a real timesaver if you've created a look you really like and want to use at other points on the page.

Apply a Format with the Format Painter

(1) In the Folder List, double-click the page you want to use.

(2) Select the text with the format you want to copy.

(3) Click Format Painter in the Standard toolbar.

(4) Select the text to which you want to apply the format. The format is "painted" automatically.

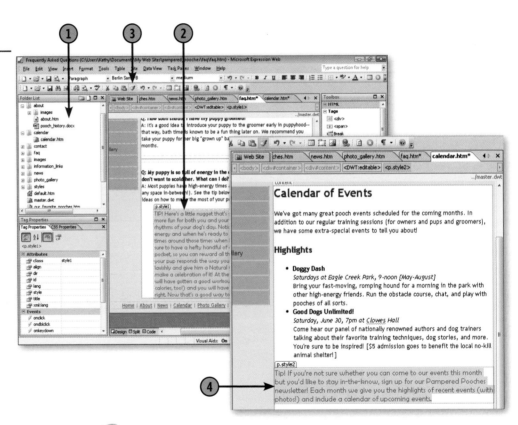

Tip

If you want to use the Format Painter at multiple points in your document, you can save time and trouble by pressing and holding the Ctrl key when you double-click Format Painter. This tells the tool to stay active until you click outside the page or press Esc to cancel it.

Tip

Can't find Format Painter? It's in the Standard toolbar. Display that toolbar by opening the View menu, pointing to Toolbars, and clicking Standard.

Applying Styles

Expression Web includes a number of ready-made styles that you can apply to various text elements on your page. The styles help you control the format of common items, like headings, lists, quotes, and more.

Apply a Style to Your Text

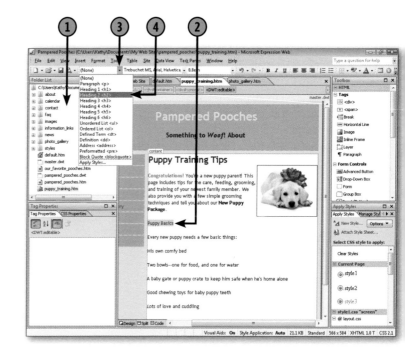

(1) In the Folder List, double-click the page you want to change.

(2) Select the text.

(3) Click the Styles arrow on the Common toolbar to display a list of available styles.

(4) Click the style you want to apply to the text.

Tip ✓

How much does format really matter? Maybe a lot, depending on the type of information you provide on your site. In general, less is more—don't overwhelm your reader with huge boring blocks of text. Keep the writing upbeat, lively, informative, and helpful; use the formatting to help move the reader's eye along on the page. A pleasant site experience will keep your readers coming back—and the format of your text will have a lot to do with setting the atmosphere.

See Also

To learn about CSS style sheets and find out how to create, modify, and manage your own styles, see "Working with Styles and Style Sheets" on page 197. That section goes into more detail about the way in which styles work to automate the formatting of your Web pages.

Expression Web Built-in Styles

Style name	HTML Code	Purpose
(None)		Applies no style to the text.
Paragraph	<p>	Used as the standard style of body text on the page.
Heading 1	<h1>	Displays text in the largest heading style.
Heading 2	<h2>	Displays text in the largest subhead heading style.
Heading 3-6	<h3> -<h6>	Shows text in heading styles of decreasing size.
Unordered List	<ul>	Displays a list style used for bullet points (not in a specific order).
Ordered List	<ol>	Shows a list style used for numbered lists, where sequence is important.
Defined Term	<dt>	Marks a selection in text.
Definition	<dd>	Indents selected text as a definition block.
Address	<address>	Formats for standard address block.
Preformatted	<pre>	Creates a preformatted tag set and preserves original spacing in text.
Blockquote	<blockquote>	Indents the selected text as a quote that appears set off from the text.

Creating Lists

The person who invented bullet points and numbered lists was probably somebody pressed for time. She wanted to get things done quickly, thank you very much, so she organized her thoughts down to the bare essentials. Bullet points and numbered lists on your pages help draw the reader's eye to the point on the page you most want them to see. They also break up long sections of text, help you summarize key points quickly, and give the readers a feeling they're getting clear information quickly and authoritatively.

List Dos and Don'ts

- Do use lists when you've got huge paragraphs of text you need to break up.

- Don't use whole paragraphs as items in your lists. Too much text kills the effect.

- Do keep your lists short—five bullet points is plenty.

- Don't include full sentences in each list item. Aim for five to seven words per bullet.

- Do include everything you need in step-by-step numbered lists.

- Don't combine too many steps into one item (it's confusing for readers).

Understand List Differences

Expression Web recognizes two types of lists on your pages: unordered lists (commonly known to us as *bulleted lists*) and ordered lists (which we refer to as *numbered lists*). Bulleted lists are lists of ideas that don't have to be in any particular order to make sense. Here's an example of each:

Unordered (bullet) list <UL>: You are creating a list of dog breeds to give owners an idea of how often their dogs should be groomed. The breeds can appear in any order on your Web page—the important thing is that they are all included. When you take a look at Code view, your unordered list will look something like this:

```
<ul>
    <li>Bulldogs</li>
    <li>Bassett Hounds</li>
    <li>Chihuahuas</li>
</ul>
```

Ordered (numbered) list <OL>: If you're telling the puppy owner how to assemble and put up a puppy gate, the owner needs to know the steps in a very definite order. Here's what that gate assembly process might look like in Code view:

```
<ol>
    <li>Snap the frame together.</li>
    <li>Attach the door at points A and B.</li>
    <li>Insert the handle at point C.</li>
    <li>Place the gate in the doorframe and tighten.</li>
</ol>
```

Create a List

① In the Folder List, double-click the page you want to use.

② Select the text you want to turn into a list.

③ Click either Bullets or Numbering in the Common toolbar.

Notice that the style changes automatically

Adding Borders and Shading

In some places on your pages you may want to make something stand out. One way you can shine a spotlight on the text on your page is to add a border to the text or slide a shade behind it.

Create a Border

① In the Folder List, double-click the page you want to change.

② Select the text.

③ Open the Format menu.

④ Click Borders and Shading.

⑤ Enter your settings and click OK.

Tip

Experiment with different looks by clicking the buttons along the sides of the Preview area to hide and display different border sides. Each button acts as a toggle; click once to hide the border; click again to display it.

Tip

You use the Padding controls in the bottom of the Borders And Shading dialog box to control the amount of space that appears between the border and the text.

Tip ✓

If you just want to apply a simple border quickly, highlight the text you want to use and click the Border tool in the Common toolbar. A palette of border choices appears; click the border style you want to apply.

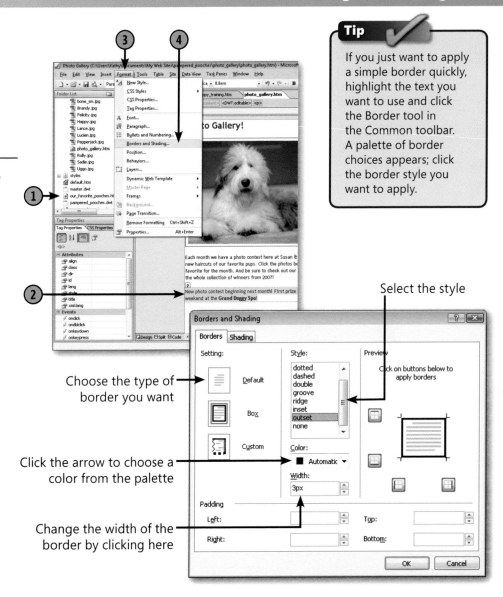

Choose the type of border you want

Click the arrow to choose a color from the palette

Change the width of the border by clicking here

Select the style

Add Shading

1. In the Folder List, double-click the page you want to change, and then select the text area you want to shade.

2. Open the Format menu and click Borders And Shading.

3. Click the Shading tab.

4. Click the Background Color arrow; choose a color from the displayed palette.

5. Click the Foreground Color arrow and click the color for the text in the shaded area.

6. Click OK.

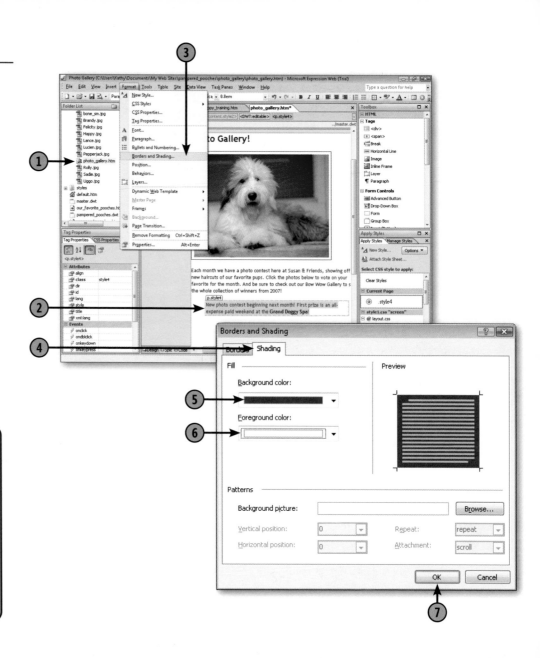

Tip

For an interesting special effect, you can apply a photo to a text selection. Display the Borders And Shading dialog box by opening the Format menu and then clicking Borders And Shading. Click the Shading tab and click the Browse button to the right of the Background Picture option. Navigate to the folder containing the image you want to use, click Open, and click OK to return to the page.

Viewing Code Changes

One of the great things about Expression Web is that you can create professional, inviting Web pages without spending a lot of time figuring out code. But if you're code reluctant, you may be pleasantly surprised to discover that it's much easier to read than you might think. Plus, Expression Web takes care of many of the details for you, ensuring that the right tags get inserted at the right places.

View Code Changes

① In a blank area of your page, type text for a heading and highlight it.

② Click Split.

③ Click the Styles arrow in the Common toolbar.

④ Click Heading 2.

... and Expression Web adds the code

Choose a style

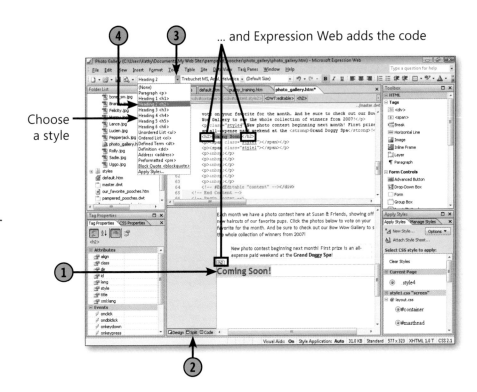

Expression Web also creates styles each time you make formatting changes on the page. The styles appear in the Current Page area of the Apply Styles task pane. You can save, rename, modify, or delete the styles that are created automatically. As your experience with Expression Web grows, this feature will enable you to create pages quickly and consistently.

An HTML Primer

HTML is an acronym for *HyperText Markup Language*, and it is the standard page description language used on the Web today. Chances are that if you've done any simple tasks on the Web—perhaps posted to a blog or added a video clip to your Windows Live Space—you've worked a little with HTML. Here are a few quick facts about HTML:

HTML tags are often used in pairs. A beginning tag <h1> and end tag </h1> tell the browser how to format the data correctly.

HTML tags can be nested within other HTML tags. For example, you might use the tag to make a word bold <strong> and </strong> in the middle of a code that has made the text another color:

<font color="red">Stanley, this is a <strong>another</strong> fine mess you've gotten me into!</font>

HTML tags can be upper- or lowercase. But because in XHTML coding (an XML-based, powerful HTML), only lowercase tagging is used, it's best to keep your tags lowercase.

Checking Spelling and Using the Thesaurus

You could design a great-looking, attention-getting, stand-out-from-the-crowd type of Web site, but one or two spelling errors on the page will leave your site visitors wondering about your attention to detail (not to mention your spelling ability!). Make sure that your text is as good as it can be by using the spelling checker and thesaurus before you turn the site loose to the masses.

Check Your Spelling

1. In the Folder List, click the topmost folder.
2. Press F7 and select Entire Web Site.
3. Click Start.

(continued on the next page)

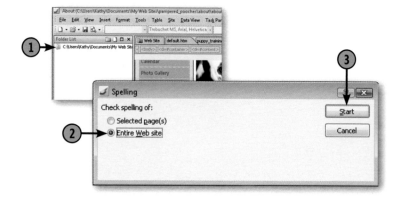

Check Your Spelling *(continued)*

④ Double-click one of the errors in the list.

⑤ Click Change to accept the corrected spelling.

⑥ Click Back To List to return to the Spelling list and finish correcting errors.

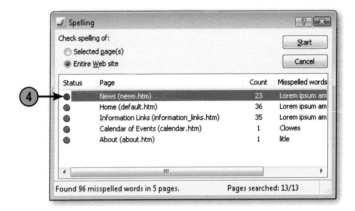

> **Tip** ✓
>
> If you just want to check the spelling of a word or phrase, select the text you want to check and press F7. Expression Web will do a quick check of the selected text and display any errors found.

> **Tip** ✓
>
> Use the Spelling Options to fine-tune the way you want the Spelling Checker to work. Open the Tools menu, point to Spelling, and choose Spelling Options. You can have Expression Web look for errors in capitalization, skip Internet addresses and words with numbers, and add custom dictionaries.

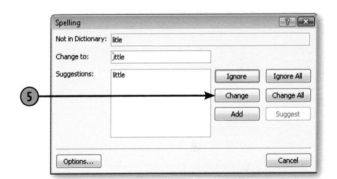

> **Tip** ✓
>
> Earlier in this section you saw that the word litle was pointed out with a little wavy underline. This happened because, by default, Expression Web checks the spelling of text you enter on the page. The little wavy line alerts you to a possible mis-spelling. This is a great feature, but if you want to turn it off, you can clear the Check Spelling As You Type check box in the Spelling Options dialog box.

Use the Thesaurus

① Select the word you want to look up.

② Open the Tools menu.

③ Click Thesaurus.

④ In the Thesaurus dialog box, select the meaning of the word.

⑤ Choose a word in the Replace With Synonym list.

⑥ Click Replace.

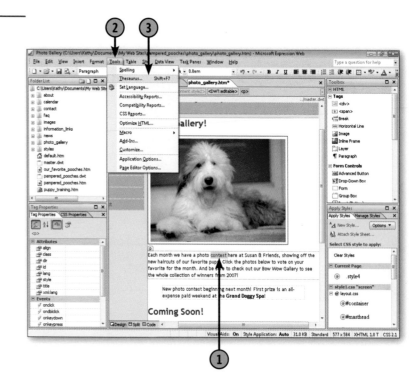

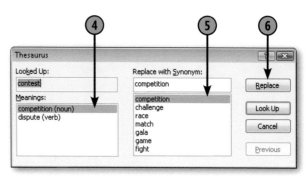

Tip

The Thesaurus is fun to work with if you're trying to add a little variety to your word choice. You can go on almost forever by clicking a word in the Replace With Synonym list and clicking Look Up. That set of words will take you to another set of words, and so on. Eventually you may wind up very far from the word you started with, but at least your vocabulary will get a boost!

Finding and Replacing Text

Any program that works with text needs to give you the ability to find and replace text. This happens all the time—a piece of information changes and you need to search out every place on your Web site where it is mentioned and replace it with something else. If you have a small site, this may not be a big

deal, but if you have hundreds of pages in your site (don't laugh—it happens!), finding one phrase used dozens of times will be a real headache. Luckily, you can avoid that hassle by using Find and Replace.

Find and Replace Choices

Feature	Purpose
Find	Searches the entire site or the current page for the word, phrase, or expression you indicate.
Replace	Finds the word or phrase you enter and replaces it with text you specify.
HTML	Searches the entire site or current page for specific tags in your site and performs a replacement action you select.

Find Text

1 Open the Edit menu.

2 Click Find.

(continued on the next page)

Find Text (continued)

③ In the Find What box, type the word or phrase you want to find.

④ Select whether you want to search the entire site or selected pages.

⑤ Select the direction for the search.

⑥ Click Find Next to find the next occurrence or Find All to display all occurrences.

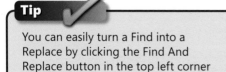

Tip

You can easily turn a Find into a Replace by clicking the Find And Replace button in the top left corner of the Find 1 window.

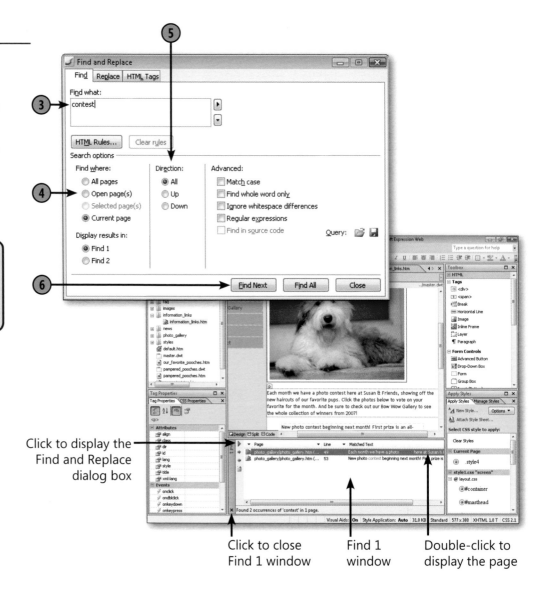

Click to display the Find and Replace dialog box

Click to close Find 1 window

Find 1 window

Double-click to display the page

Replace Text

① Display the Replace tab of the Find And Replace dialog box by pressing Ctrl+H.

② In the Find What box, type the text you're looking for.

③ In the Replace With box, type the text you want to insert.

④ In Find Where, select whether you want to replace the text in the entire site or on selected pages.

⑤ Click Replace All.

Tip

Because HTML tags are very important for the right display of your page, it's important to take a little extra care when searching and replacing HTML tags. The third tab in the Find And Replace dialog box, HTML Tags, provides you with the choices you need to search for specific tags and let Expression Web know what to do with them when they're found. For example, you might want to find the <address> tag and remove the tag and any contents associated with it throughout the whole site. In the HTML Tags tab, you would select Address in the Find Tag list and Remove Tag And Contents for Replace Action. Click Replace All to finish the task.

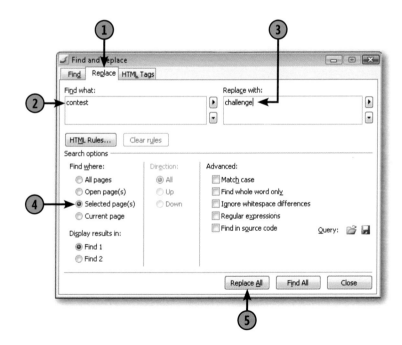

Moving On

This section covered a lot of ground, introducing you to the various ways you can add and work with text on your Web pages. Before moving on to the next chapter, take some time and get comfortable adding, editing, and enhancing the text on your pages. Try adding a few paragraphs, headings, and block quotes. Put your story on the page! Nobody else can say it like you can. The next section shows you how to bring your words to life by adding and working with pictures.

6

Working with Pictures

We live in a visual world. Think of the beauty of spring, a mist over the mountains, the bright orange of wildflowers opening in the morning sun.

The early days of the Web were all about the text, but today's Web is about experience—oh, and information, too. The savvy visitors of your Web site come there with a purpose, but they will expect a certain type of experience once they arrive.

The pictures on your Web pages really have two purposes. Perhaps first and foremost, they will give the reader's eye a rest and liven things up on your page. In addition to the aesthetic value, pictures have functional worth. Using a picture, you can show your visitors what your product looks like, or where your home office is located, or how happy people are when they are connected with you. Pictures inspire, and pictures of people—especially happy, smiling, or peaceful people—send the message, "Here is something good." And that's a feeling you'd like to have your visitors to have when they visit your site, right?

This section gives you all the steps you need for adding images to your Web pages. Expression Web makes it all very simple. You don't need to use code at all to make pictures look great on your pages.

Getting Ready to Add Pictures

The first step in adding pictures to your pages involves making those pictures available in Expression Web. Although you don't have to import the images before you use them, when you use the Import feature to add pictures to the Folder List, you make those files available whenever you open that Web site. Then you can simply drag and drop the pictures on the page.

Add Pictures to the Folder List

① Select the folder in the Folder List where you want to add the picture.

② Open the File menu.

③ Point to Import, and then click File.

(continued on the next page)

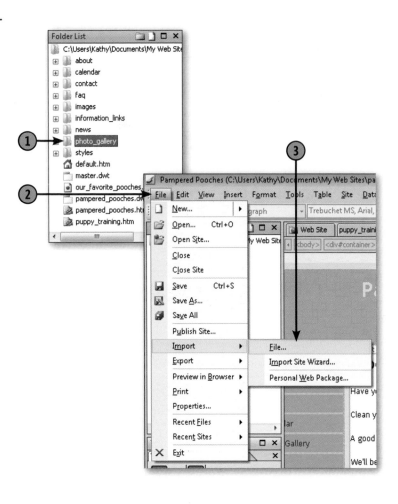

Tip

Add to the Folder List when there's a chance you'll want to use the pictures on multiple Web pages. Once files are added to the Folder List, you can drag the files to any page in the current site.

If you created your Web site using one of Expression Web's Dynamic Web Templates, a folder named images is already created for you. You can use this folder for your pictures or create and use any other folder you choose. To create a new folder, click the New Folder tool in the top right side of the Folder List title bar.

Add Pictures to the Folder List *(continued)*

④ In the Import dialog box, click whether you want to import pictures as individual files, in a folder, or from an existing site.

⑤ Click OK to add the files.

Tip

When you add an entire folder of images (by clicking Add Folder in the Import dialog box, selecting the folder you want, and clicking Open and then OK), the folder is copied into the Folder List along with all the files that it contains. You can rename the folder if you choose by right-clicking the folder in the Folder List, clicking Rename, and entering a new name for the folder. Press Enter or click OK to change the name.

Tip

If you choose to import files from an existing site, the Import File Wizard launches and you can choose the site from which you want to download the files. You can download files from any standard Web site, a folder on your computer or local network, or an FTP site.

Tip

When you add picture files to the Folder List, you can simply drag and drop them on the page. When you import pictures one by one, you'll use the Import Picture from the File tool in the Common toolbar.

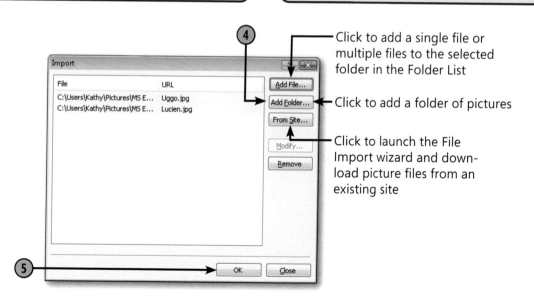

Click to add a single file or multiple files to the selected folder in the Folder List

Click to add a folder of pictures

Click to launch the File Import wizard and download picture files from an existing site

Importing vs. Embedding Pictures

If you'd prefer to import a new image each time you add a picture, that's fine, too, but it creates a little wrinkle you may have to deal with later. When you use the Import feature to add the pictures to the Folder List, the picture files are automatically stored with all the elements used on your Web pages. So when you save the site and prepare it for publishing on the Web, Expression Web has everything it needs. When you import a picture file, Expression Web will embed the image in the page, which works. But if anything ever happens to the image, or it is corrupted on the page and doesn't display, Expression Web won't be able to access the original file in order to fix the problem.

Understanding Picture Types

The pictures you add to your Web site need to be one of three types in order for them to show up on your pages: JPEG, GIF, or PNG. Of these three types of files, JPEG is the most common—it's the format your digital camera uses to save the photos you capture. GIF pictures are popular on the Web because they load quickly and can be read by all browsers, but they are typically simple art and don't give you the same range of color you would get with a photo saved in JPEG or PNG format. PNG is a relatively new format that is designed to bring you the best of both GIF and JPEG format. Each format has its pros and cons. The trick is in choosing the right format for the type of art you're putting on your page. Here's a quick look at how these formats compare:

GIF format
22.3 KB

JPEG format
11.1 KB

PNG format
137 KB

 Tip

Don't be afraid to experiment with the different picture types. Your main objective is to use the best looking (that is, highest quality) picture you can without overloading your page with huge pictures that appear slowly.

Picture Type Comparison

Type	Stands for	Benefits	Limitations
JPEG	Joint Photographic Experts Group	High quality, Great for photos, Can be compressed and maintain quality	Lossy compression style
GIF	Graphics Interchange Format	Small file sizes, Lossless compression, Fast downloads	Limited to 256 colors
PNG	Portable Network Graphics	High quality, Lossless compression, Support for 16 million colors	Larger file size than JPEG for photos

More about File Types

You may be wondering about the file types you already have—the ones created automatically by your favorite devices and programs. Here's a quick list:

- Digital photos are typically JPEGs.

- Digital video files straight from your camera are MPEGs. Video files you download maybe in MPEG, AVI, WMV, or other formats.

- Clip art downloaded from the Web is often saved in GIF or PNG format.

- Files created in a paint program, such as Windows Paint, can be saved in a number of formats: WMP, PCT, TIF, JPEG, GIF, and PNG.

- Files created in an illustration program, like Microsoft Expression Design, can be saved in numerous formats (WMP, PCT, TIF, JPEG, GIF, and PNG).

Tip

The terms lossless and lossy compression are technical terms that really point to something simple. PNG and GIF formats are considered lossless compression styles—this means that the pictures in those formats can be compressed with no loss of quality. JPEG, on the other hand, is a lossy compression style. This means that when you compress a JPEG file, perhaps compressing a digital photo so that it appears faster on your Web site, you won't be able to reverse the compression and return the image to its previous high quality. Once it's compressed, pixels are thrown out with the trash, and that's that. If you think you might want to reverse the compression of a favorite JPEG, save the file in the PNG format (using your favorite image editor) before adding it to your page.

Tip

The term file extension refers to the characters that follow the dot (.) in the file name. File extensions are not just an unimportant part of the file name you can change to anything you like—programs read the file extension to determine whether a specific file is saved in a format the program can open. For best results, leave the file extension of any picture file (or document file, for that matter) as set by the program in which it was created. Then you don't have to deal with any unwanted surprises when Expression Web says, "File not found," when you know the blasted thing is right there in the folder where you put it.

Create Professional Images with Expression Design

Throughout this book we're focusing on Expression Web, but that program has a sister you need to know about. Microsoft Expression Design is the professional illustration program included in Microsoft Expression Studio, enabling you to create top-of-the-line images and graphic designs that work seamlessly with Expression Web. Here is a list of some of the high points in Expression Design:

■ Powerful vector drawing tools. (A vector image is a type of art that is created based on mathematical calculations. A line art diagram is one example of a type of vector art. Vector images can be reshaped, resized, and modified in any way with no loss of quality.)

■ A huge palette of editing tools

■ Integration of vector and bitmap images. (A bitmap image is a type of art that is created by painting individual pixels with certain colors. A photograph is one example of a bitmap image.)

■ A gallery of special image effects

■ Easy export capabilities

■ Integrates smoothly with other programs in Expression Studio

Expression Design is available as a stand-alone product or as part of the Expression Studio (which includes Expression Web, Expression Design, Expression Blend, and Expression Media). To find out more about Expression Design, go to *www.microsoft.com/expression/products/overview.aspx?key=design*.

Adding Pictures

Now that you've added your pictures to the Folder List in Expression Web, you're ready to place them on the page. Expression Web gives you two choices for the way you do this.

The simple method is to drag and drop a picture onto the page. The other simple method involves using the Import Picture From File tool on the Common toolbar.

Drag a Picture to the Page

1. Click to expand the folder in the Folder List containing the picture you want to add to the page.

2. Click the picture you want to add.

3. Drag the picture to the page and release the mouse button.

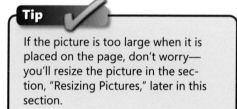

Tip

If the picture is too large when it is placed on the page, don't worry—you'll resize the picture in the section, "Resizing Pictures," later in this section.

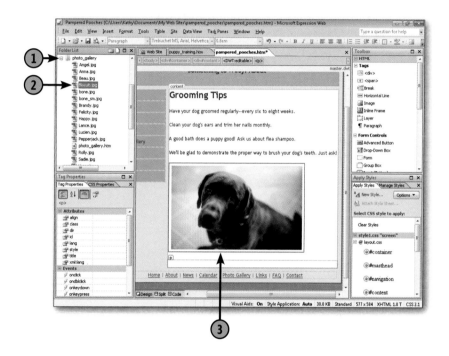

Place a Picture on the Page

① Click at the point on the page where you want to add the picture.

② Click the Insert Picture From File tool on the Common toolbar.

③ Navigate to the file you want to add and select it.

④ Click Insert.

⑤ In the Alternate Text box, type text that you want to appear while the image is downloading.

⑥ Click OK.

Tip ✓

Always provide alternate text to let users know what the picture shows while they are waiting for it to download. Alternate text also describes the image in the event that the picture file is damaged or unable to download.

Tip ✓

The alternate text you add for your pictures is something that search engines notice when they are scouring the Web for results, so be sure to use this to your advantage. Do make sure that the text you use really does reflect what's in the image, though. (It's not nice to fool Mother Search Engine.)

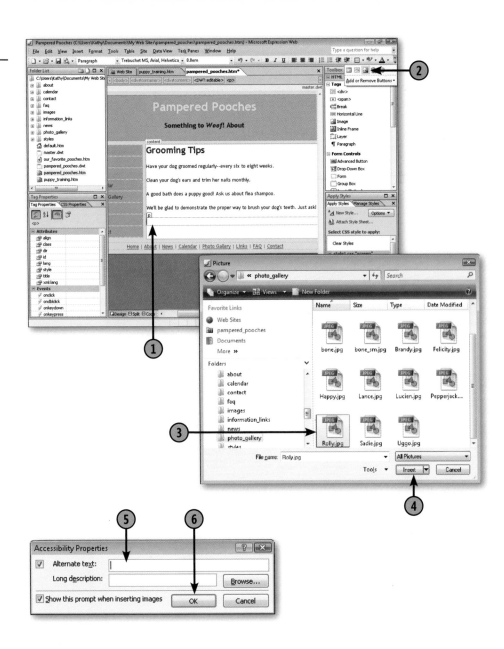

Resizing Pictures

When you first add a picture to your page, the text may move unexpectedly to a new point on the page. If the picture is too large for the width of the page, the text and the picture move to a wider spot on the page. You can correct this and return the text to its proper position by resizing the picture.

Drag a Picture to Resize

① Click the picture you want to resize.

② Position the pointer on a picture handle and drag it in the direction you want to resize the picture.

HTML tag placed in code

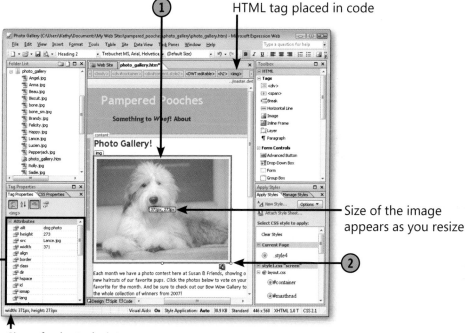

Picture attributes

Size of the image appears as you resize

Size of selected picture

Resize Precisely

(1) Right-click the picture you want to resize.

(2) Click Picture Properties.

(3) Click the Appearance tab.

(4) Specify the width and height (in pixels) or the percentage values for the picture.

(5) Select Pixels or Percent.

(6) Click OK.

Tip ✓

When you're working in Design view, you can display additional choices by clicking the Picture Actions button that appears along the lower right edge of a selected picture. You can choose Only Modify Size Attributes or Resample Picture To Match Size. These two options control whether additional settings related to the picture style and settings are changed when you resize the picture.

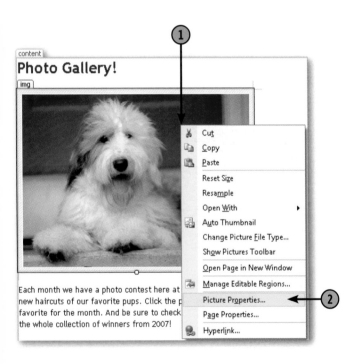

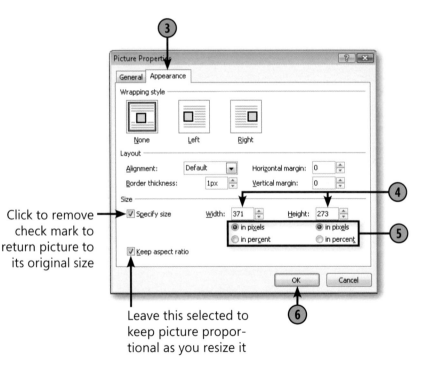

Click to remove check mark to return picture to its original size

Leave this selected to keep picture proportional as you resize it

Controlling Picture Placement in Text

Expression Web gives you three basic choices for the way in which the text flows around the pictures on your page. You can position a picture on the left side of the page so all text wraps around it on the right; you can plop the image in the center of the page so the text skips the picture and continues below it; or you can snuggle it up against the right margin, so all text flows around it on the left.

Choose Text Wrap

① Right-click the picture you want to change.

② Click Picture Properties.

③ Click the Appearance tab.

④ Select the text wrap style you want to apply (None, Left, or Right).

⑤ Click OK.

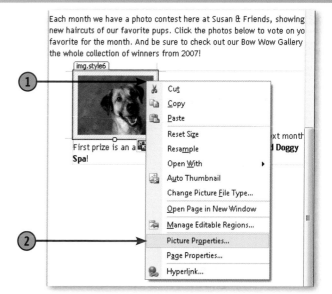

Tip

You can choose a different text wrap setting for each picture on your page. From a design standpoint, varying the picture placement is a good idea (it adds visual interest to the page), unless you're creating a catalog-style page that requires a specific format (for example, all pictures on the left and all descriptions on the right).

Tip

If you're having trouble getting your text to wrap evenly around the picture on your page, check the Appearance tab of the Picture Properties dialog box. Chances are that the Wrapping Style setting is set to None or the Alignment setting is set to a value that is keeping your picture from doing what you want it to do.

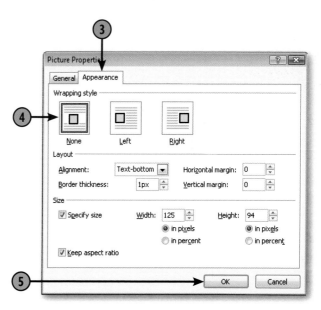

Aligning Pictures

Expression Web gives you several different choices for the way you align a picture in the paragraph in which it is placed. For example, you might want to display a thumbnail picture aligned with the top of the text. To do this, you use the Alignment option in the Appearance tab of the Picture Properties dialog box.

Align a Picture

① In the Picture Properties dialog box, click the Appearance tab.

② Click the Alignment arrow.

③ Select your choice from the displayed list.

④ Click OK.

Tip

If you have the Wrapping Style setting set to None, the Alignment setting you select may not act the way you expect it to. Before choosing the alignment for your picture, make sure you've made the Wrapping Style choice.

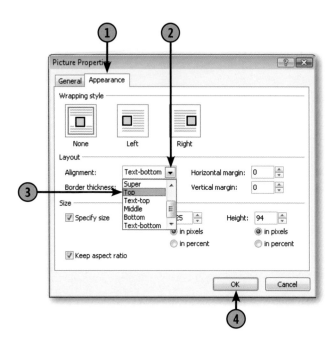

Adding Picture Margins and Borders

When you first add a picture to your page, you will notice that there's not a lot of room between the image and the text; in fact, one seems to run right up against the other. You can add some padding around the pictures on your page by increas- ing the margin values in the Picture Properties dialog box. To make your picture stand out even more, you can add a border to set it off from surrounding text.

Add Spacing around Pictures

(1) In the Picture Properties dialog box, click the Appearance tab.

(2) In the Layout area, increase the Horizontal Margin and Vertical Margin values by clicking the up arrows to the right of the settings.

(3) Click OK.

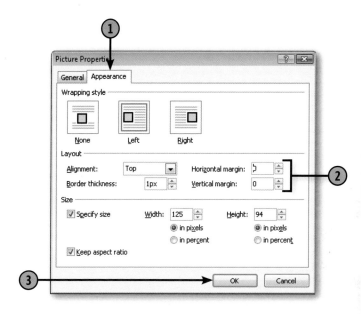

Tip ✓

It may seem counterintuitive to create a Web page and then be careful about how much content you put on it. You're pay-ing for it, right? You might as well use the medium to convey as much information to the visitor as possible. On a purely informational level, it does make sense to put as much as you can in front of a viewer, but on the experiential level, we know that people turn off mentally (which means "click away," on the Web) when they are overloaded with data. So, as strange as it may seem, remember that blank space is one of the most important elements you can add to your page—room for the reader to take a break, to help the reader see clearly where one element ends and another begins, room for the items on your page to breathe.

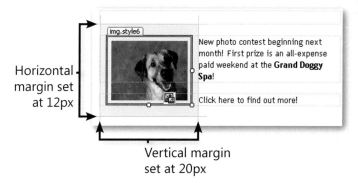

Horizontal margin set at 12px

Vertical margin set at 20px

Create a Picture Border

① In the Picture Properties dialog box, click the Appearance tab.

② Click the Border Thickness arrow to increase the setting value (the higher the number, the thicker the border).

③ Click OK.

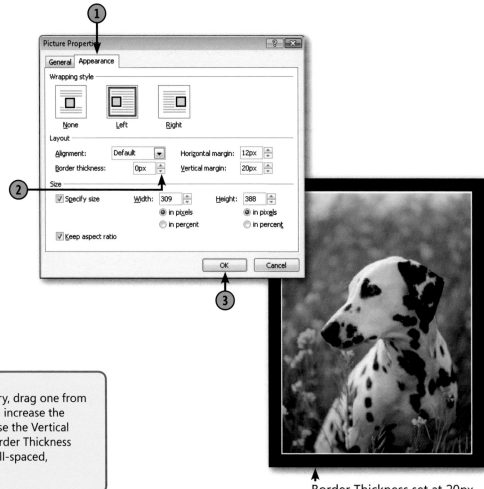

Border Thickness set at 20px

Try This!

Right-click a picture on your page (if necessary, drag one from the Folder List). Click the Appearance tab and increase the Horizontal Margin value to 10px. Now increase the Vertical Margin value to 16px. Finally, increase the Border Thickness value to 10px. Click OK. Now you've got a well-spaced, bordered picture.

Editing Pictures

In addition to all the placement, spacing, and border choices you can make for your pictures, you can do some actual image editing in Expression Web. Expression Web includes a Pictures toolbar that provides all the tools you need for correcting brightness and contrast problems, rotating pictures, setting the display order and layering of items, and much more.

Display the Pictures Toolbar

① Open the View menu.

② Point to Toolbars.

③ Click Pictures.

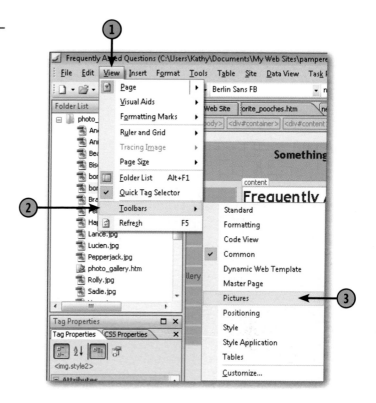

Tip

The Pictures toolbar is a floating toolbar, which means it appears on top of your workspace. You can "dock" the toolbar so that it stops floating if you like. Simply drag it toward any edge of the workspace window and it will add itself along the margin as a new toolbar row.

Tools for Image Editing

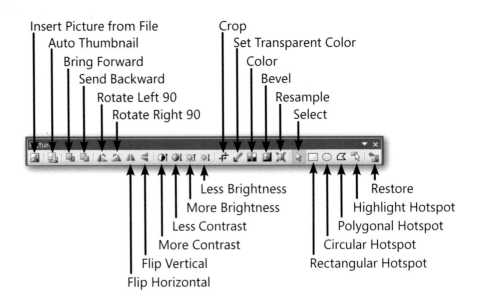

Insert Picture from File
Auto Thumbnail
Bring Forward
Send Backward
Rotate Left 90
Rotate Right 90
Crop
Set Transparent Color
Color
Bevel
Resample
Select

Less Brightness
More Brightness
Less Contrast
More Contrast
Flip Vertical
Flip Horizontal
Restore
Highlight Hotspot
Polygonal Hotspot
Circular Hotspot
Rectangular Hotspot

Picture Tools—Which to Use When

When You Want To...	Use...
Make a dark image lighter	More Brightness
Make a fuzzy picture sharper	More Contrast
Turn a picture on the page	Rotate Left 90, Rotate Right 90, Flip Vertical, or Flip Horizontal
Add a picture saved on your computer	Insert Picture from File
Cut out unnecessary parts of a picture	Crop
Change the coloring in a picture (or make it black and white)	Color
Create a thumbnail of a picture	Auto Thumbnail
Display the picture on top of (or behind) another item on the page	Bring Forward or Send Back
Make a picture look like a clickable button	Bevel
Let page elements "show through" the picture	Set Transparency Color
Add a hotspot to a picture	Rectangular Hotspot, Circular Hotspot, or Polygonal Hotspot
Return the picture to its original state	Restore

Cropping Pictures

One of the most important things you can do to really make your pictures great involves pruning them back to the most important images in the picture. This technique is known as *cropping*. Expression Web includes a crop tool that enables you to cut away the parts of the picture that aren't essential to the overall message or feeling you want to convey.

Crop a Picture

1. Click the picture you want to change.

2. Click the Crop tool on the Pictures toolbar.

3. Click the crop handles on the picture and drag them to enclose the area of the picture you want to keep; then press Enter.

Tip

Click the Restore tool on the Picture toolbar to undo any changes you made to the picture since you last saved the Web page.

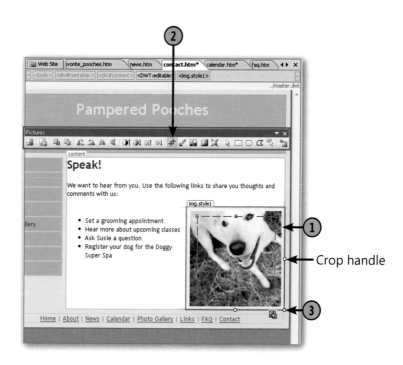

Crop handle

Color on the Web

As you learned earlier in this section, the different picture formats handle colors differently. Both JPEG and PNG formats can display more than a million different colors. That's one of the reasons they are great for photographs. GIF format, on the other hand, is limited to displaying only 256 colors.

One of the challenges in creating something that looks good on the Web is that people use different types of computer hardware and software—and you don't have any control over that. Some folks who visit your site are still using the same RGB monitor they bought in the early '90s; others will have state-of-the-art monitors they purchased recently. Different hardware (and different browsers running on that hardware) means that the green on your monitor may be much different from the green displayed on a monitor around the corner or around the world. With a whole world full of differences, how can you be sure your visitors are seeing what you want them to see?

Something called a *Web-safe palette* is one answer to this dilemma. This is a collection of colors that are guaranteed to be consistently displayed on all browsers everywhere. The trouble with the Web-safe palette is that it includes only 256 colors, not the huge range JPEGs and PNG formats are capable of displaying. To see the colors included in the Web-safe palette, go to *www.techbomb.com/websafe/*.

Today's Web user is unlikely to suffer from an overexposure to colors outside the Web-safe palette, however, and in many cases you may notice no difference at all on different monitors. If you want to be extra safe and ensure that your colors are as true as possible, use a Web-safe color for your page background, headers, and font colors, and go ahead and use JPEGs and PNG files for your pictures.

Creating an Auto Thumbnail

Expression Web includes a great feature that enables you to create thumbnails of your pictures so they don't take up a lot of room on your page. Visitors to your site can then click the thumbnail to expand it in the browser window. Expression Web creates the link and does the resizing for you. All things should be so simple.

Add an Auto Thumbnail

① Drag the picture from the Folder List to the page.

② Right-click the picture.

③ Click Auto Thumbnail.

Tip

Because thumbnails are such small images, you need to be sure your picture is in good shape before turning it into a thumbnail. Crop the image as needed and use Expression Web's picture editing tools to fix any problems in brightness or contrast before you create the thumbnail.

Preview an Auto Thumbnail

- Click the Preview arrow in the Common toolbar.

- Select the browser you want to use from the displayed list.

- In the Web browser, click the thumbnail of the picture. The picture appears in a larger size in the browser window.

Click to display the picture in a large size

Viewing Pictures in Code

When we started this session, I mentioned that you can add pictures to your pages and make them look good without ever working with any code at all. That's true, but it's not a bad idea to keep an eye on what's happening behind the scenes as you work in Design view. You can also add pictures (or create placeholders for pictures you'll add later) by using the Image tool in the HTML Toolbox.

Create an Image Object from the Toolbox

① In the Folder List, double-click the page you want to change.

② Click Image in the Toolbox and drag it onto the page.

③ Position the image object where you want it to appear and release the mouse button.

Tip

You may want to add image placeholders when you don't yet have the pictures you plan to use on the page. You can go ahead and set size, margin, text wrapping, and margin settings for the pictures, even through the images haven't been added yet.

Replace an Image Placeholder with a Picture

① Double-click the image placeholder.

② Click Browse and choose the picture you want to use.

③ Click OK.

Click Browse and navigate
to the folder containing the
picture you want to use,
select it and click Open

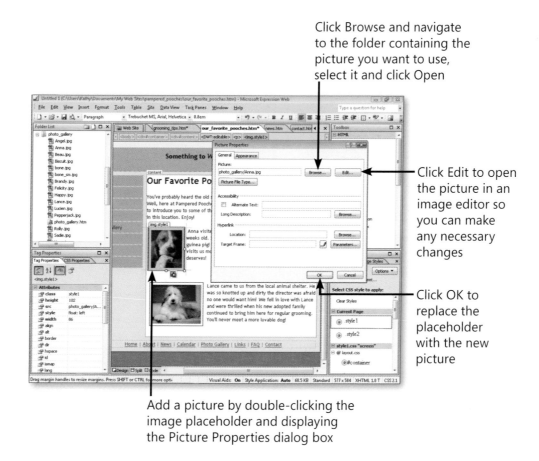

Click Edit to open
the picture in an
image editor so
you can make
any necessary
changes

Click OK to
replace the
placeholder
with the new
picture

Add a picture by double-clicking the
image placeholder and displaying
the Picture Properties dialog box

View Image Code

① Click a picture on your page.

② Click Split at the bottom of the Editing window.

③ Review the <img src> code highlighted in the top pane.

The image attributes appear both in the code and in the Tag Properties task pane

Try This!

Select a picture on your page and click Split. Locate the <img src> line (it should be highlighted) in the Code window at the top of the screen. Find the width setting and add 100 to that number; then press F5 to refresh the screen. What happened? Most likely, the picture now looks all out of whack. To fix it, select the picture again, and this time locate the Width setting in the Tag Properties task pane. Remove the 100 you previously added and click outside the Width box. The picture should be back to normal now. What a relief.

Tip

One of the great things about Expression Web is the way everything is interrelated. You can easily change something about one of the pictures on your page by changing a value in the Tag Properties task pane or entering something new in Code view. The change will appear instantly in all three areas—in Design view, in Code view, and in the Tag Properties task pane.

Saving Pages with Pictures

The process of saving your Web pages is simple whether or not you have added pictures to your pages, but depending on the way in which you added those pictures (whether you added them to the Folder List or simply inserted them one by one), you need to tell Expression Web how you want the pictures to be saved.

Save an Embedded Picture

1. Right-click the tab of the page you want to save.
2. Click Save. The Save Embedded Files dialog box shows a list of all embedded pictures.
3. Click the Picture File Type button.
4. Select the file type for the picture.
5. Click OK.

Tip

If you want to change the picture settings—for example, to modify the quality settings of the image—select the Use Image As Is check box to remove the check mark. The Quality setting and the Progressive Passes settings become available and you can change those values as necessary. For most of your uses, however, Use Image As Is should be fine.

Tip

If you choose GIF as the picture file type for the embedded image, you will be able to choose whether the image should be Interlaced (which displays the picture in bands from top to bottom) or you want to make the image transparent.

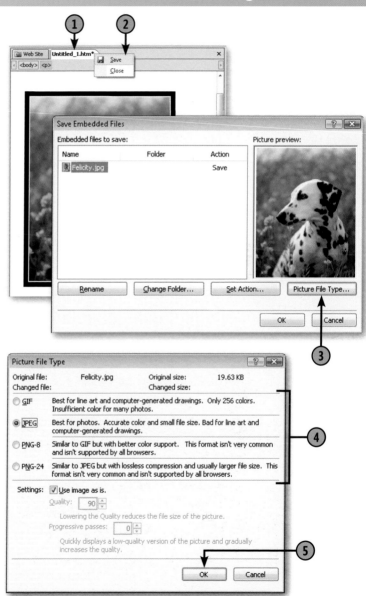

Moving On

This section covered a lot of colorful ground by showing you how to add, resize, modify, and arrange the pictures on your Web pages. The next section helps you connect the dots by creating links that will enable site visitors to move freely around your site.

7

Creating Links

Links are the magic of the Web. Without links (also called *hyperlinks*), you would have no way to get from one page to another. When you typed a search phrase into Windows Live Search and clicked the Go button, nothing would come up. When you visited Amazon.com (to buy all your friends a copy of this book), you wouldn't be able to click a link in order to get to the book page (which would be a sad, sad day for us at Microsoft Press!).

Without links, people who really need the information on your site won't be able to see it. New visitors will never find you. Only those people who have been given your e-mail address could go directly to your solitary, standalone little page. And once there, they wouldn't be able to send you an e-mail, move to another page, browse a catalog, or sign up for your services.

I'm sure you get the idea. Links are what make the Web, *the Web*.

This section shows you how to add this link magic to your blossoming Web pages. You'll be pleased to know that there all kinds of ways to add links of all sorts on your pages, which increase your chances of having the kind of impact you want to have on the Web.

Understanding Links

The concept of the link is simple. It is the code that tells the browser where to go when the link is clicked. What you may not know is that there are many kinds of links you can add to your Web site.

Links of All Kinds

Type of Link	Description
Text link	The most common type of link, applied to selected text (typically a word or phrase).
Picture link	A link applied to part or all of a picture, diagram, button, or other graphical element.
Hotspot	An area on a picture that functions as a link. In Expression Web you can create rectangular, circular, or polygonal hotspots.
Internal link	A link that connects to another page or a resource (picture, style sheet, or document) in current Web site.
External link	A link that connects to a Web page outside the existing site.
Absolute link	A link that includes the full path name of the link.
Relative link	A link that includes a partial path name, perhaps the folder and file name of the page.
E-mail Address	A link that opens a new message window so the user can send an e-mail message.

What Makes a Good Link Good?

At first glance, you might not think there's any big secret to creating effective links. But there's more to it than simply creating the physical link. A good link makes sense to your site visitors and leads them where they want to go. Ultimately, in order for a link to be effective, users have to be able to find it, know it's what they want, and click it. Otherwise, they may click away from your page. Here are a few tips for making the most of the links on your page:

A good link is easy to find. Don't stray too far from traditional link colors. Most experienced Web surfers are accustomed to seeing blue used for unclicked links, purple for clicked links, and perhaps a third color when they hover their mouse over the link.

A good link does what users expect it to do. Typically, clicking a link takes a user to a new page. Alternatively, a link may open a dialog box (so users can download a file, for example) or a mail window. Visitors can see clearly that the link took them where they expected to go. If you link back to items on the same page (known as *in-page links*), visitors may get confused and think the link didn't take them anywhere. If you need to use that kind of link, spell it out clearly in the surrounding text.

A good link lets you know what's coming. If your link takes a visitor to a dialog box that gives them the choice of opening or saving a file, tell them so before-hand. Same goes for opening a PDF. Assume that your Web visitors will expect your links to take them to a new Web page—and if the link does anything different, be sure you explain that to visitors before they click.

A good link uses consistent language. If you are consistent with the terms you use on your site and in your links, visitors will have an easier time finding their way around. If your link says, "Click here to see our fall schedule," be sure that somewhere in the first few lines on the target page, visitors will see the words "fall schedule." Otherwise, they might think they've landed on the wrong page.

A good link connects to something worthwhile. Search engines care what you link *to*. Links that link to other relevant sites are given more weight than links that go off to something random. The reason? Internet search engines are concerned with relevancy. Make sure the pages you link to make you look good. Your site will be lifted in the search results (or dropped, as the case may be) by the company it keeps.

Tip

If you used a Dynamic Web Template to create your site, Expression Web creates all the pages, adds pictures, and inserts links for you. The links that enable the pictures to show up on the page and connect the various pages in the site are known as *internal links*.

Adding Links to Text

Visit any page on the Web and you are almost certain to find a number of text links. Most may be headlines, teasers, or links to other pages (depending on the type of site you visit).

Others may be links that take you to a Web form or a contact page, or links that open an e-mail window.

Create a Text Link

1. Click the page that you want to add the link to.

2. Select the text for the link.

3. Click the Insert Hyperlink button in the Common toolbar.

(continued on the next page)

Tip

The trouble with "Click here" links is that they don't say much. They don't tell your site visitors what they are going to see when they do click the link; but even worse, they don't give the search engines any information to work with when they scour your site for relevant information. If at all possible, include a good search term in the link. It just might bring a larger audience to your site.

Create a Text Link *(continued)*

④ Choose whether you want to display files in the current folder, Web pages you've recently viewed, or files you've recently worked with.

⑤ Select the page you want to link to.

⑥ Click OK.

Click to navigate through folders

Use to browse the Web to find the page you need

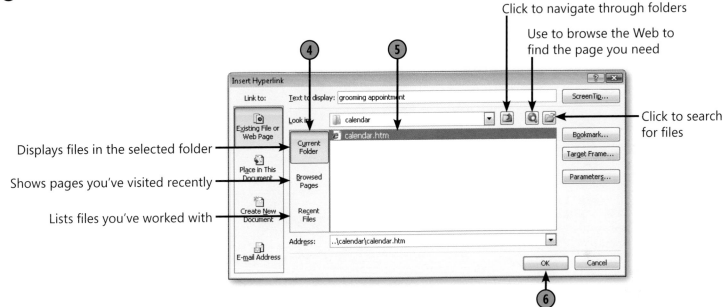

Displays files in the selected folder

Shows pages you've visited recently

Lists files you've worked with

Click to search for files

Try This!

You don't have to choose a Web page from the list in the Look In box in order to connect with a page outside of your site. If you know the URL, simply type it in the Address box and click OK.

Know Your Search Terms

Before you create links that will bring boatloads of visitors to your site, you need to know what people are looking for. (This kind of research helps you determine which keywords to add to your pages, too.) Here are a few online tools you can use to find out what people are searching for. Then you can experiment with the terms you hope will bring people to your site:

The Keyword Selector Tool enables you to enter a word or phrase you're considering and see how many people searched on that term (and related terms) in the last month. To try out the tool, go to *http://inventory.overture.com/d/searchinventory/suggestion/*

Try out Google's Keyword Tool to test out your search terms and get suggestions for additional phrases that may increase your site traffic: *https://adwords.google.com/select/KeywordToolExternal*

Use Google Hot Trends to see what people are searching for on a daily—or even hourly—basis. Here's the link: *www.google.com/trends/hottrends*

Viewing Links as Code

Adding links is a simple matter when you use the Insert Hyperlink dialog box. Expression Web does the rest of the work behind the scenes. You can view, change, move, and remove the link by working in Design, Code, or Split views.

View the Link as Code

1 Highlight the link you've just created.

2 Click Split.

(continued on the next page)

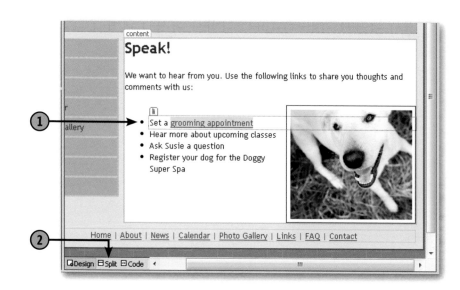

View the Link as Code *(continued)*

③ Find the highlighted phrase in the Code window at the top of the screen.

④ Click Design to return to Design view.

The code for
the added link **③**

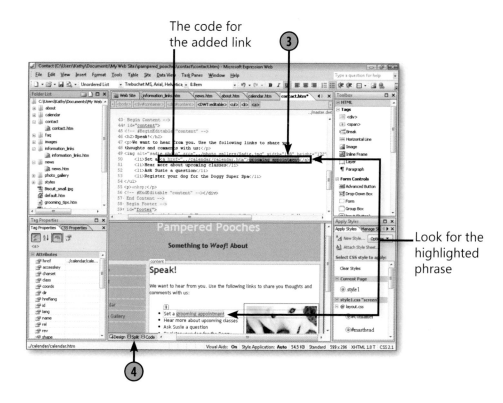

Look for the
highlighted
phrase

Anatomy of a Link

Whether you create a text link, a picture link, a hotspot, or a bookmark, the basic code for adding a link is similar. Every link begins with an opening angle bracket, followed by the A HREF tag and an equal sign (=). The path to the resulting page (the page displayed when the link is clicked) appears in quotation marks, followed by the closing angle bracket.

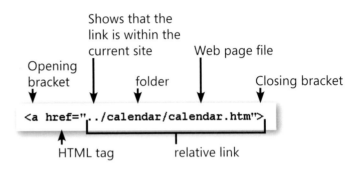

Shows that the link is within the current site

Opening bracket

Web page file

folder

Closing bracket

`<a href="../calendar/calendar.htm">`

HTML tag

relative link

Caution

This example shows a relative link that links to another file in the same site. If you are linking to a page on the Web outside your site, you will need to use the full URL (for example, *http://www.microsoft.com*).

Adding Links to Pictures

If you are showcasing your products online, tempting visitors with great vacation spots, or inspiring users to try your workout classes, you can add links to your pictures so users can simply click them to go where their interests lead them. Expression Web makes it easy for you to use the whole picture as a link or create hotspots that turn a portion of the picture into a live link.

Create a Picture Link

① Right-click the picture you want to add the link to.

② Click Hyperlink.

(continued on the next page)

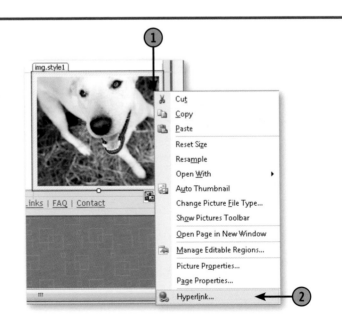

Create a Picture Link *(continued)*

③ Navigate to the folder containing the page you want to link to.

④ Click the page.

⑤ Click OK.

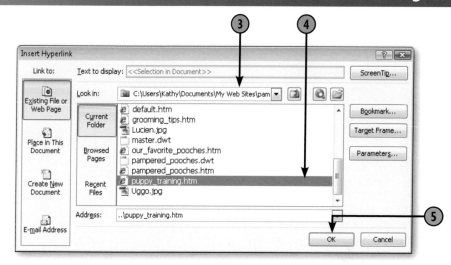

Create a Hotspot

① Select the picture you want to use.

② Open the View menu.

③ Point to Toolbars.

④ Click Pictures if it is not already selected.

(continued on the next page)

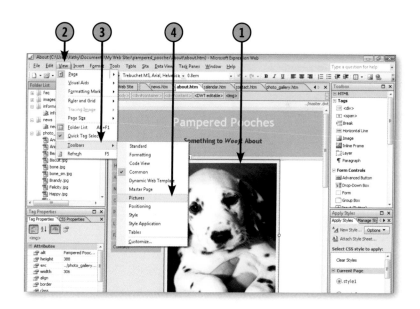

Create a Hotspot *(continued)*

⑤ Click the Hotspot tool you want to use.

⑥ Click and drag a shape for the hotspot on the picture.

⑦ Click the page you want to link to.

⑧ Click OK to add the link to the hotspot.

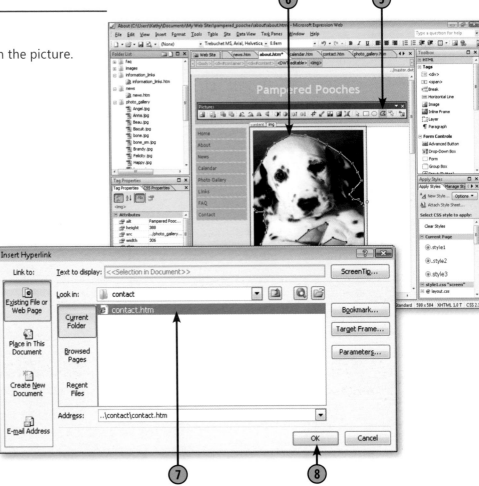

Tip ✓

If you click the Circular Hotspot tool, the pointer changes to the shape of a pencil. The point at which you click to draw the hotspot will be the center of the hotspot, so be sure to click in the center of the area you want to select.

Tip ✓

If you select the Rectangular Hotspot tool, the pencil pointer appears. When you click to begin drawing the hotspot, the point you click will serve as the upper left corner of the hotspot area. Drag the pointer down and to the right to create a rectangular hotspot.

Tip ✓

Use the Polygonal Hotspot tool when you want to choose an irregular shape for the hotspot. This is a fun tool when you want to outline specific items on the picture and link them to different things.

Adding a Link to an E-mail Address

Another type of link doesn't lead to another Web page at all; instead, it opens a new message window so that visitors to your site can send you an e-mail message. The process of adding this hyperlink is similar to the ones you've already seen, with a few minor differences.

Create an E-mail Link

① Select the text you want to use as the e-mail link.

② Open the Insert menu.

③ Click Hyperlink.

④ Click E-mail Address.

⑤ Enter the e-mail address for the link.

⑥ Click OK.

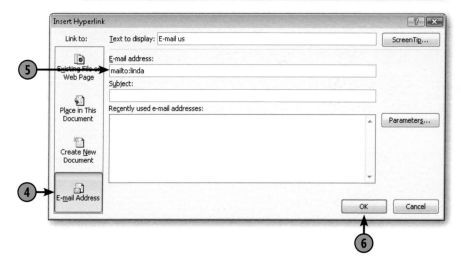

Tip

You can set the Subject line to include a specific phrase so you know that the user has clicked a link on your site. For example, on the Groomers page of the Pampered Pooches page, the e-mail link automatically inserts *Grooming info* in the subject line.

Inserting Bookmarks as Links

Bookmarks on your Web page can act as anchors for links on your page. You might, for example, add a bookmark at the beginning of a section where you want visitors to go to sign up for an upcoming class. At the appropriate point on the page, you can create a link that takes the visitor to that bookmark.

Add a Bookmark to Your Page

① Click on the page where you want to add the bookmark.

② Open the Insert menu.

③ Click Bookmark.

④ Type a name for the bookmark.

⑤ Click OK.

Tip

You can display the Bookmark dialog box quickly by pressing Ctrl+G.

Tip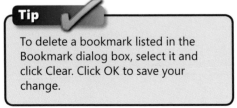

To delete a bookmark listed in the Bookmark dialog box, select it and click Clear. Click OK to save your change.

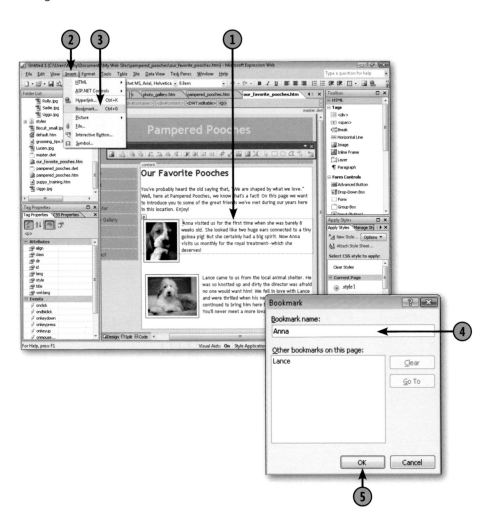

Create a Link for the Bookmark

① Select the text you want to link to the bookmark.

② Click the Insert Hyperlink tool in the Common toolbar.

③ Click Bookmark.

④ Select the bookmark of the destination you want.

⑤ Click OK.

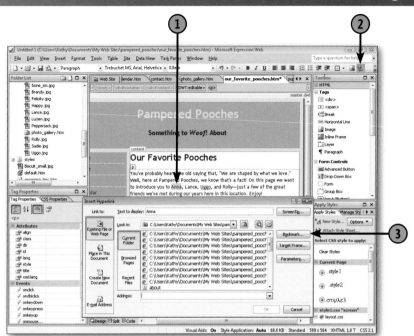

See Also

In addition to text and picture links, you can add buttons and navigation bars to your Web pages to help visitors find their way around. To learn about adding these interactive elements to your pages, see Section 11, "Adding Interactivity," starting on page 185.

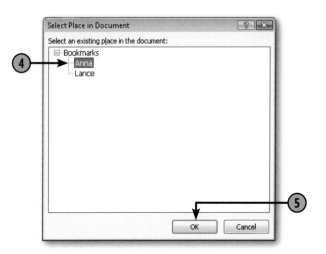

Adding a ScreenTip to a Link

Web sites seem friendlier when users know what to do while they're visiting. You can take the guesswork out of navigating your site by adding ScreenTips to key links. A ScreenTip displays a pop-up text box when the user hovers the mouse over the link.

Create a ScreenTip

① Select the link you want to change.

② Right-click the selection and click Hyperlink Properties.

③ Click ScreenTip.

④ Type the text you want to add as a ScreenTip.

⑤ Click OK.

Tip

A good ScreenTip is concise, direct, and tells users either what to do next or where a link will take them.

Try This!

Add a ScreenTip to a link to tell visitors more about the link. Highlight the link and right-click it. Click Hyperlink Properties. In the Edit Hyperlink dialog box, click ScreenTip. Type the text you want users to see when they position the mouse pointer over the link. Click OK.

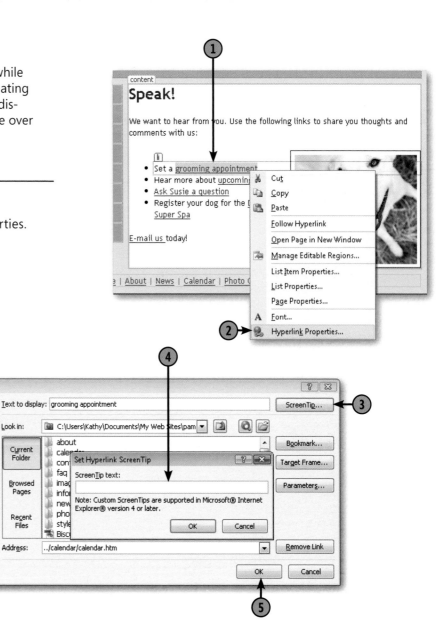

Changing the Look of Links

By default the links you create will appear in blue, but you can easily change the color if you want the links to coordinate with the other colors you've used on the site. (If you want to leave the links in that bright blue to make them stand out on the page, that's okay, too.) Expression Web actually gives you four different chances to choose colors for your links, depending on the state of the link. Sound like mumbo-jumbo? Read on for a quick explanation.

Understanding Link States

Link State	Description
Hyperlink	The natural state of the hyperlink before a user has clicked it.
Visited Hyperlink	The user has clicked the hyperlink and returned to the page. A new color lets the user know that the link has already been followed.
Active Hyperlink	The state of the hyperlink as the user selects it.
Hovered Hyperlink	The state of the hyperlink when the user positions the mouse pointer over it.

Change Link Color

1. Display the page with the links you want to change.
2. Open the File menu.
3. Click Properties.

(continued on the next page)

See Also

If you have created your Web site by using a Dynamic Web Template, the Hyperlink settings in the Formatting tab of the Page Properties dialog box will be disabled, meaning you won't be able to change them. To modify the link states, you'll need to use the procedure in the next section, "Modifying Link Styles."

④ Click the Formatting tab.

⑤ Click the arrow of each link state
you want to change and choose
the color from the displayed
palette.

⑥ Click OK.

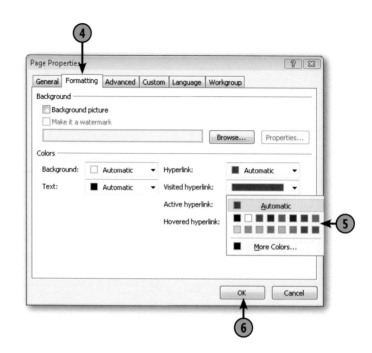

Modifying Link Styles

You'll learn more about working with CSS in "Working with
Styles and Style Sheets" on page 197, but for now I want to
call your attention to a change in CSS style you've already
made without knowing it. When you change the color of
links on a page, Expression Web creates four new styles and
displays them in the Manage Styles task pane. You can change

more than the color of hyperlinks by modifying the styles in
the Manage Styles task pane. You might want to remove the
underline, or display the link in a different font (which isn't
usually recommended because it can look a bit jarring on
the page).

Change Link Style

1. In the Manage Styles task pane, right-click the style you want to change.

2. Select Modify Style.

3. In the Modify Style dialog box, change the settings for the style.

4. Click OK.

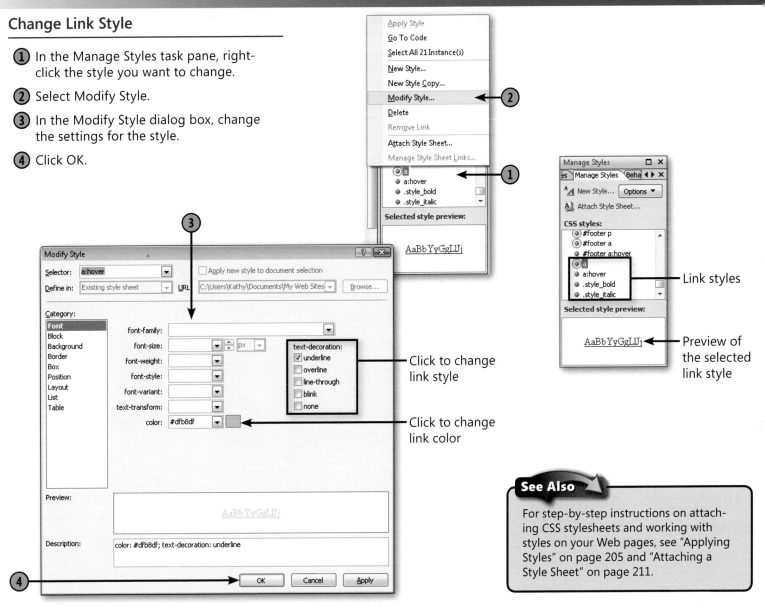

Apply Style
Go To Code
Select All 21 Instance(s)

New Style...
New Style Copy...
Modify Style... ← ②
Delete
Remove Link

Attach Style Sheet...
Manage Style Sheet Links...

a
a:hover
.style_bold
.style_italic

Selected style preview:

AaBbYyGgLlJj

Modify Style

Selector: a:hover

Define in: Existing style sheet   URL C:\Users\Kathy\Documents\My Web Sites   Browse...

Category:
Font
Block
Background
Border
Box
Position
Layout
List
Table

Apply new style to document selection

font-family:
font-size: px
font-weight:
font-style:
font-variant:
text-transform:
color: #dfb8df

text-decoration:
☑ underline
☐ overline
☐ line-through
☐ blink
☐ none

Click to change link style

Click to change link color

Preview:

AaBbYyGgLlJj

Description:

color: #dfb8df; text-decoration: underline

OK   Cancel   Apply

Manage Styles

Manage Styles   Beha

A New Style...   Options ▼

Attach Style Sheet...

CSS styles:
#footer p
#footer a
#footer a:hover
a
a:hover
.style_bold
.style_italic

Link styles

Selected style preview:

AaBbYyGgLlJj

Preview of the selected link style

See Also

For step-by-step instructions on attaching CSS stylesheets and working with styles on your Web pages, see "Applying Styles" on page 205 and "Attaching a Style Sheet" on page 211.

Displaying Links

You can go to a lot of trouble to create great looking links on your site, but if they aren't working properly, they aren't going to do anybody any good. Expression Web includes Hyperlinks view so that you can see all the links connected to your page, coming and going.

View Page Links

① Display the page with the links you want to see.

② Open the Site menu.

③ Click Hyperlinks.

④ Click the + to display the links for additional pages.

Tip

If you'd rather see page titles than file names, right-click the view and click Show Page Titles.

Tip

To display only the picture links for the selected page, right-click a blank spot on the page and click Hyperlinks to Pictures.

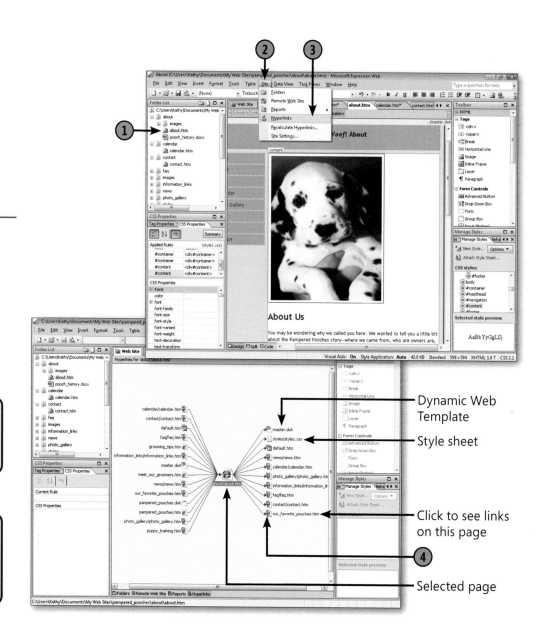

Dynamic Web Template

Style sheet

Click to see links on this page

Selected page

Checking and Repairing Links

The more your Web site grows, the more likely it is that a link may get changed or broken. Expression Web gives you a simple way to do a quick check of all the links on your page and repair the ones that need it.

Test Your Links

① In the Folder List, click the page you want to view.

② Open the Task Panes menu.

③ Click Hyperlinks.

④ Review the links in the Hyperlinks task pane.

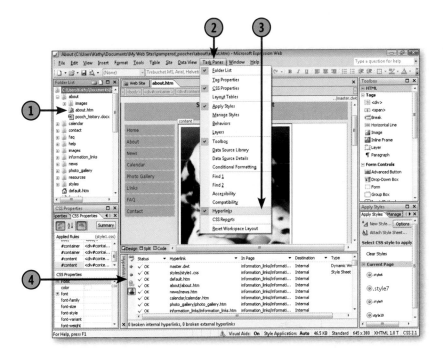

Edit or Repair Links

① In the Hyperlinks task pane, double-click the link you want to edit.

② To change the link on the page, click Edit Page, or

③ To replace the link with a new page, click Browse and choose the page you want to use.

④ Choose whether to make the change in all pages or selected pages.

⑤ Click Replace.

See Also

Expression Web enables you to create reports that make it easy to troubleshoot problems with links and missing files. To find out more about generating reports for your site, see "Creating a Site Report" on page 230.

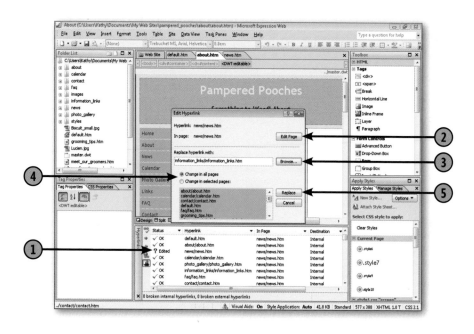

Moving On

This section showed how you to create a Web of easy-to-navigate pages by adding text, pictures, bookmarks, and e-mail links on your site. The next chapter tackles a more specialized (but still not difficult) form of information display: the almighty, ever-functional table.

8

Adding Tables

If you're the kind of person who likes to put socks in one drawer and t-shirts in another, chances are that you like tables. I think most of us have some kind of driving organizing principle that enables us to relax when things are put together logically. Chaos no longer rules. Tables in Expression Web enable you to present your site visitors with information in a quick-look format. If you design the table well, readers will know at a glance what the columns mean, what the rows are telling them, and why you decided to put this information in a table in the first place.

Expression Web makes it easy to create some really nice tables. You won't be applying lots of bells and whistles like drop shadows and animation effects and such (who wants that in a Web table anyway?); but simple, clean, and orderly are good. In this section, you learn about the two different tools Expression Web gives you to use as you add tables to your pages. You'll be able to do the whole thing—start to finish—in minutes. I promise.

Understanding Tables and Layout Tables

Once upon a time, not so long ago, the only way trustworthy Web designers could get large collections of data to line up on the page was to put that data in tables. Tables provided boundaries that the blank Web page just didn't have. Today, with the advent of style sheets (which you'll learn about in "Understanding Styles" on page 200), we have a new kind of container to house our data so that it doesn't go spilling out all over the page. But tables are still popular, and here's why: they provide a special kind of structured display for data you want your site visitors to understand quickly.

Introducing Table Types

Expression Web enables you to create two kinds of tables. Each has a different *raison d'etre* (reason to be) on your Web page.

Table	Type	Description
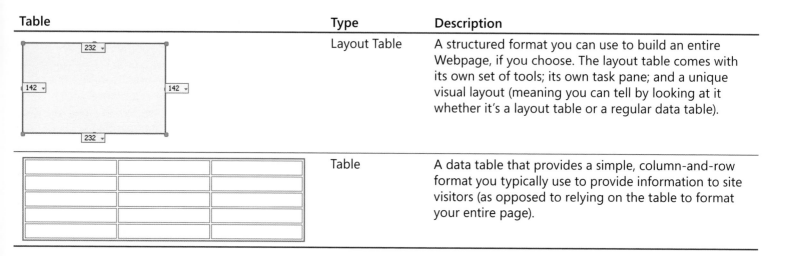	Layout Table	A structured format you can use to build an entire Webpage, if you choose. The layout table comes with its own set of tools; its own task pane; and a unique visual layout (meaning you can tell by looking at it whether it's a layout table or a regular data table).
	Table	A data table that provides a simple, column-and-row format you typically use to provide information to site visitors (as opposed to relying on the table to format your entire page).

Adding a Layout Table

A layout table offers precision for those times when you want to control how and where your data flows on the page. Begin by displaying the Layout Tables task pane. That's where you'll find the tools to start the process.

Create a Layout Table

1. Create a blank page by clicking New in the Common toolbar.
2. Open the Task Panes menu.
3. Click Layout Tables.
4. Click Insert Layout Table.

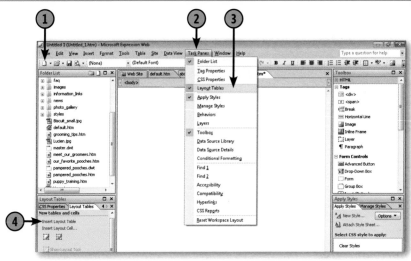

Choose a Layout Style

1. Scroll to the bottom of the Layout Tables task pane.
2. Scroll through the layouts in the Table Layout box.
3. Click a Table Layout.

Tip

How do you know which layout works best for your site? Think about where you want the navigation panel to go. What about your site logo? What will your page header look like? And where do you want visitors to look first? Answering these questions will help you decide which of the ready-made layout table styles will best fit the page you're creating.

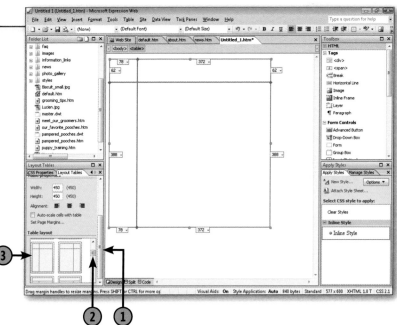

Insert Cells

1. Click in the layout table where you want to add the cell.
2. Click Insert Layout Cell.
3. Set the Width and Height.
4. Choose whether you want the cell to appear before or after the selection.
5. Click OK.

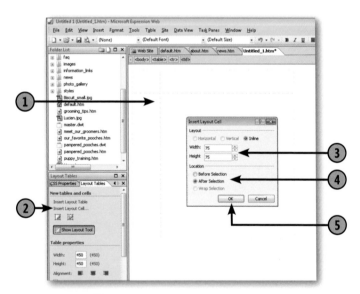

Align the Layout Table

1. Select the layout table.
2. Scroll the Layout Table task pane to display the Alignment options.
3. Click the Alignment you want for the table.

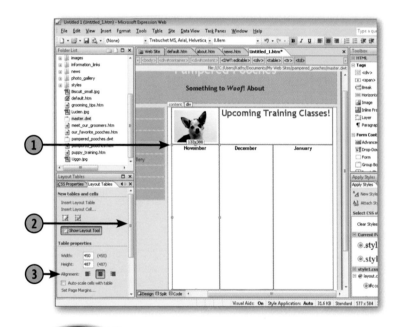

Tip ✓

Even though layout tables are designed to give you an added measure of precision over the display of your data, you want the information to scale naturally if the table is resized. To do that, click the Auto-Scale Cells with Table check box in the Layout Tables task pane.

See Also

Although you create layout tables and regular tables by using different methods, once they are created they are similar. You can format, resize, copy, and work with layout tables and regular tables using the same techniques. You'll find techniques for arranging, enhancing, and previewing your tables later in this section.

Resizing a Layout Table

When you want to change the size and shape of layout table cells—or the layout table as a whole—you can choose one of two ways to do it:

- To change the size of the entire layout table, change the Height and Width settings in the Layout Tables task pane.

- To change the size of a specific layout table cell, click the edge of the cell and drag it in the direction you want to resize the cell.

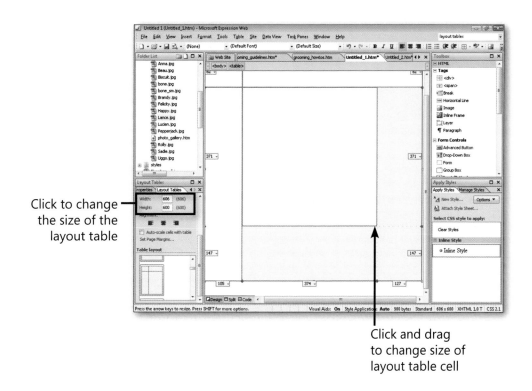

Click to change the size of the layout table

Click and drag to change size of layout table cell

Creating a New Table

In essence, a table is a simple, elegant thing. Each row gives you information about something—a breed of dog, a type of haircut, a brand of food. Each column provides the individual pieces of data about the item in the row. Visitors to your site can gather information quickly by scanning the rows in a table. They don't have to work as hard—or read as much—to find out what they need to know. And that ease of use leads to a better Web experience, which leads to happy visitors, which leads to—well, you know what: more people coming back to see you, and bringing their friends. This section shows you how to create a simple data table for your Web page.

Add a Table

(1) Click the page where you want to add the table.

(2) Open the Table menu.

(3) Click Insert Table.

(4) Type the number of rows and columns for the table.

(5) Choose the alignment and spacing settings.

(6) Indicate table border settings, if desired.

(7) Choose a background color or picture, if desired.

(8) Click OK.

Tip ✔

If you really like the table you're creating here and want to use it as the basis for other tables you create in this site, select the Set As Default for New Tables check box.

Tip ✔

If you want to display the Layout Tools automatically when the table is created, select the Enable Layout Tools check box in the Insert Table dialog box. This adds a layout grid, with column and row sizes, to the table you create so that you can adjust the layout of the table easily.

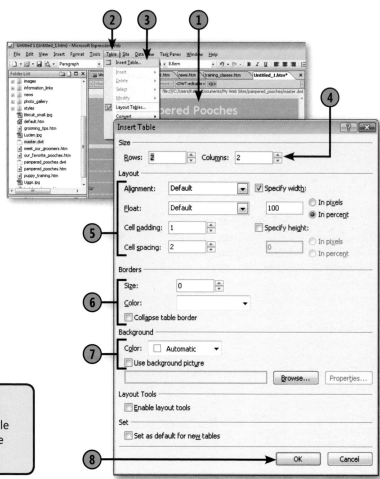

Adding Table Data

There's something fulfilling about adding well-organized information into little modular cells on a page. Here's how to add
data to the table you've just created.

Enter Table Data

① Type the label for the first column in the table and press
Tab; continue entering data as needed.

② Highlight the first row and press Ctrl+B to make the
column headings stand out (optional).

Grooming Schedule

Groomer	Mon	Tue	Wed	Thu	Fri	Sat	Sun
Bev	8-3	off	8-12	off	8-12	off	closed
Todd	8-12	td	off	off	off	8-3	closed
Lisa	off						

See Also

Notice how the cell expands automatically when you type?
Yes, you guessed it—you'll need to do some resizing in a
minute. Luckily that's the topic of the next section.

Tip

If you selected Enable Layout Tools in the Insert Table dialog
box, you won't be able to move from cell to cell in the table by
pressing Tab. To enter data in a layout table, you need to click
each individual cell and then type the information for that cell.

Tip

To turn off Layout Tools, right-click the table, click Table Properties, and clear the Enable Layout Tools check box. Click OK to
save the change.

Simple Table Navigation

Press...	To Do This...
Tab	Move the cursor one cell to the right.
Shift+Tab	Move the cursor one cell to the left.
Down-Arrow	Move the cursor down one cell.
Up-Arrow	Move the cursor up one cell.

Tip

Have a lot of repeating data? You can use the Fill command
(available in the Table menu) to fill table cells quickly. Start by
selecting the table data you want to use to fill the table; then
open the Table menu, and point to Fill. Depending on whether
you've selected column data or row data, the Fill command
provides you with Down or Right (or both). Click the direction
you want to fill and Expression Web does the rest.

Adjusting Column Width

After you add data to the table, it will probably be obvious that a little resizing is in order. You can adjust your table column widths several different ways, but however you choose to do it, it's a pretty simple task.

Change Column Width

① Select the column you want to resize by clicking the top edge of the column heading cell.

② Position the pointer on the right edge of the column, and click and drag the column to resize as needed.

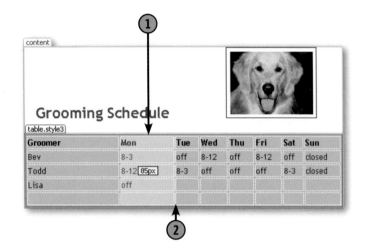

Tip

Notice that the column width appears when you click the column. This is helpful when you want to resize a number of columns so that they are all the same size.

Tip

You can display (and change) more information about individual cells by right-clicking a selected cell, column, or row and clicking Cell Properties. The Cell Properties dialog box enables you to change all sorts of things about the selected cells—layout, borders, background, column width, and row height.

Try This!

To make a number of columns the same width, select two or more columns on your table, right-click the selection, and click Cell Properties. In the Cell Properties dialog box, select the Specify Width check box. Click in the Specify Width box and type the width (in pixels or percentage) you want those columns to be. (Use percentage if you want the selected columns to use a specific percentage of space in the table.) Click OK to save your settings and the columns are resized accordingly.

Working with Table Tools

A sculptor needs a good set of tools in order to produce a masterpiece. Similarly, you need a set of easy-to-use tools if you're going to be up to your elbows in table data. The Table

Toolbar contains a full set of tools that enable you to add and remove columns, align data, format cells, and much more.

Display the Table Toolbar

① Open the View menu.

② Point to Toolbars.

③ Click Tables.

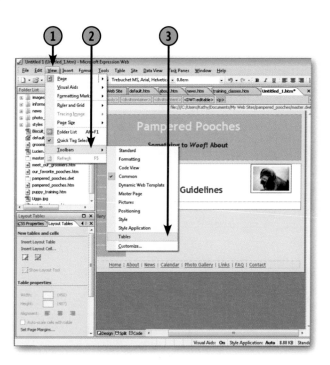

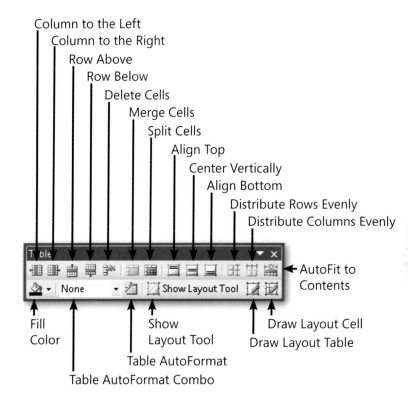

Column to the Left
Column to the Right
Row Above
Row Below
Delete Cells
Merge Cells
Split Cells
Align Top
Center Vertically
Align Bottom
Distribute Rows Evenly
Distribute Columns Evenly

AutoFit to Contents

Fill Color
Show Layout Tool
Draw Layout Cell
Draw Layout Table
Table AutoFormat
Table AutoFormat Combo

Adding, Deleting, and Moving Rows and Columns

By now you know that creating a table is pretty simple—nothing tricky about it. Tweaking the table to display the data you want in just the right order sometimes involves adding, removing, or reordering rows and columns.

Add a Column or Row

1. Click the top edge of a column or the left edge of a row; when the column or row is highlighted, right-click it.

2. Point to Insert.

3. Select the item that best reflects where you want to add the column or row.

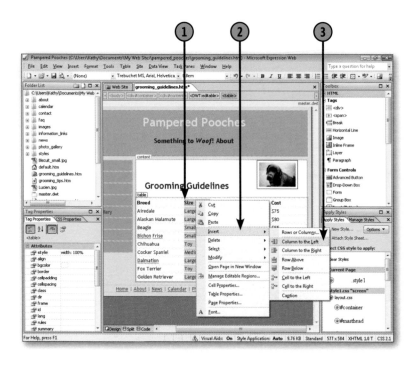

Tip

If you want to add more than one row or column at a time, right-click in the row or column beside which you want to add the rows or columns. Point to Insert, and click Rows or Columns. In the Insert Rows or Columns dialog box, click whether you want to add rows or columns, specify how many, and decide where you want the columns to be placed. Click OK to add the number of rows or columns you specified.

Try This!

Select a row in your sample table by clicking and dragging the mouse pointer over the row. Right-click the selection. Point to Insert and click Row Below.

Delete a Row or Column

① Click the left edge of the row or the top of the column you want to delete and right-click it.

② Point to Delete.

③ Click Delete Rows.

Tip

If you choose to delete individual cells instead of rows, start by selecting the cells you want to delete; then right-click the selection, point to Delete, and click Delete Cells. Be forewarned though—the cells are deleted immediately after you click the command; you aren't asked to confirm the deletion. (The saving grace is that you can press Ctrl+Z to undo your action if you suddenly realize you've made a horrible mistake.)

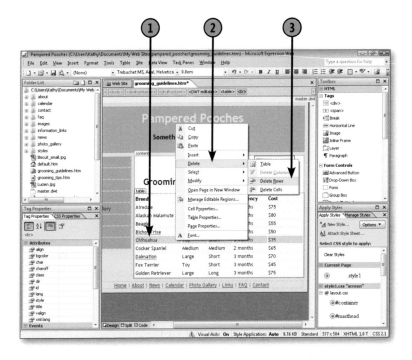

Cut and Paste a Column or Row

① Select the column or row you want to move and right-click it.

② Click Cut.

③ Select the column to the left of where you want to pasted column to appear. (If you're moving a row, choose the row above the pasted row.) Right-click the selection.

④ Click Paste.

Tip

You can also use the old standard shortcut keys—Ctrl+X for Cut and Ctrl+V for Paste (plus Ctrl+C for Copy)—when you are working with table data.

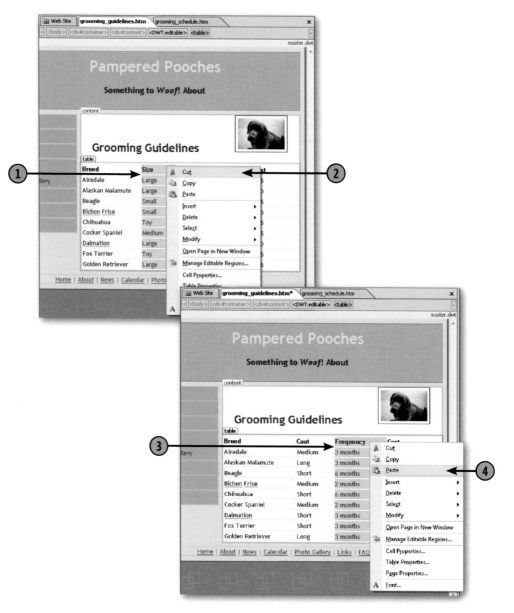

Merging and Splitting Cells

In some cases, after you create your table, you may realize that it makes more sense to have two cells of data combined into one (for example, perhaps you don't need both a first name *and* a last name column) or to split one cell into two. Expression Web makes this a simple task.

Split Cells

① Highlight the cells you want to split and right-click the selection.

② Point to Modify.

③ Click Split Cells.

④ Choose whether you want to split the cells into columns or rows.

⑤ Enter the number of columns or rows you want to contain the split data.

⑥ Click OK.

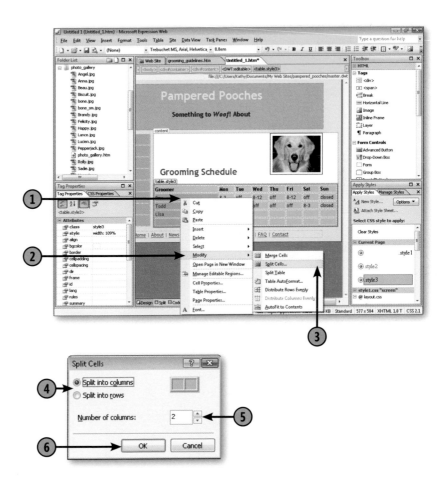

Tip ✓

When would you want to split cells? Dividing up your data is helpful for site visitors when you have put several items together in a single cell or the table cells are difficult to read.

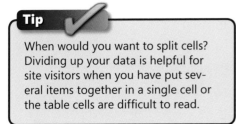

Merge Cells

① Highlight the cells you want to merge and right-click the selection.

② Point to Modify.

③ Click Merge Cells.

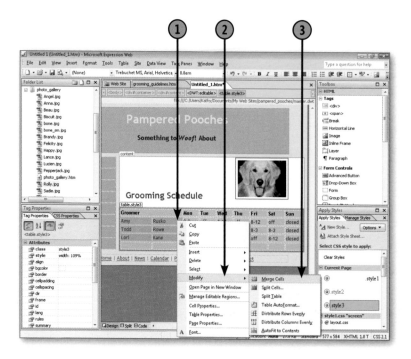

Tip

Your merged cells may need a little editing before you are ready to continue. You might need to add a space between data items, adjust the width of the column, or move things around before finishing your table.

Caution

Note that Expression Web will merge into one cell as many cells as you care to select. This means that if you select multiple columns and rows (thinking you might merge two entire columns into a single column), you will wind up with one cell (not one column) with a lot of data!

Wrapping Text around a Table

A table can be a great addition to a page, especially if you're trying to display a lot of information in a reasonably ordered fashion. But in order for the table to look good on the page, it needs to play nicely with the text surrounding it. Here's how to make sure text wraps around your table the way you want it to.

Wrap Text Around a Table

1. Right-click the table.
2. Click Table Properties.

3. Click the text wrapping option you want.
   - Default doesn't use a text wrapping feature;
   - Left positions the table along the left margin so that text wraps on the right;
   - Right positions the table on the right margin so text wraps to the left.
4. Click OK.

The table and text cohabitate nicely on the page, making a more enjoyable page viewing experience for everyone.

Formatting Tables

The way your table looks on the Web really is just as important as the quality of information it contains. If it is boring, packed with information, or difficult to use, you can bet that people aren't going to give it a second glance. To make sure that your table attracts the attention you want it to get, a little formatting is in order. You'll make your formatting changes in the Table Properties dialog box.

Enhance the Table with Table Properties

① Right-click the table.

② Click Table Properties.

③ Choose the settings you want to apply to the table.

④ Click OK.

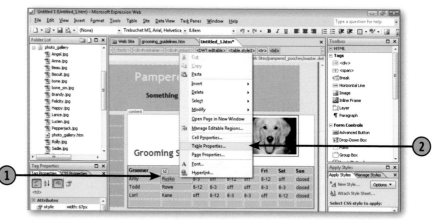

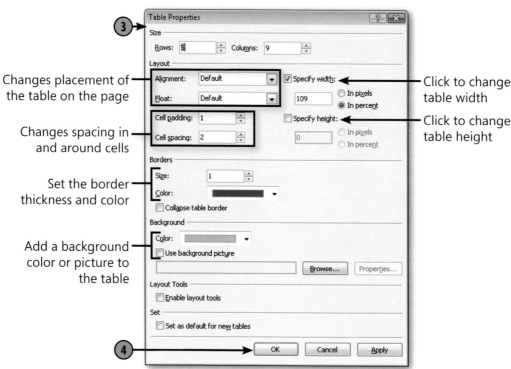

Changes placement of the table on the page

Changes spacing in and around cells

Set the border thickness and color

Add a background color or picture to the table

Click to change table width

Click to change table height

What a Difference a Setting Makes!

Result	Table Property Setting
	Cell padding set to 10
	Cell spacing set to 10
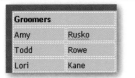	Border set to 10
	Background picture added

Distributing Table Content

Depending on the type of data you're showcasing in your table, the data entries may be similar in length or they may be widely different. Having some entries that are long and wordy and others that are just a few words can look a little unwieldy. (So much for uniformity.) But you can improve the overall look of the table and space everything out nicely by using a couple of commands Expression Web provides.

Distribute Table Content Evenly

① Select the table columns or rows you want to change and right-click the selection.

② Click Modify.

③ Click the option that best fits the way you want to distribute the content.

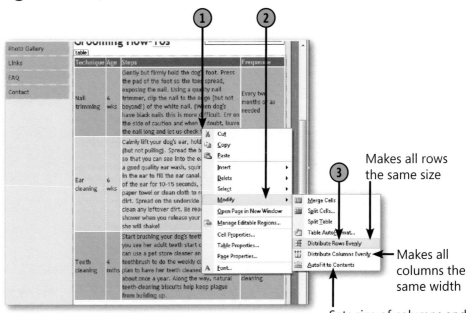

Makes all rows the same size

Makes all columns the same width

Sets size of columns and rows automatically based on content

Viewing Table Code

Even though Expression Web makes it possible for you to create great looking pages without ever having to deal with code at all, it's a good idea to know what you're looking for when you need to find the HTML that actually produces the table on the page. Here's how to find your table in Code view and tweak it if necessary.

Display Table Code

1. Right-click the table.
2. Click Select.
3. Click Table.
4. Click Split.

Tip

You can easily make changes in Code view if you like. If, for example, you decide that you want to change the "Frequency" column heading to "How Often?" you could change it in Code view by highlighting Frequency (shown in line 63 in the example) and typing How Often? The text is changed automatically on the page in Design view.

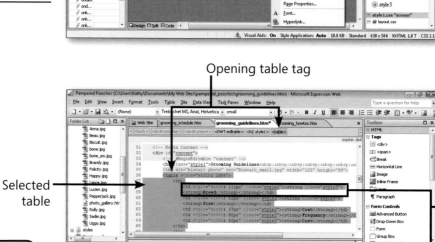

Opening table tag

Selected table

Format and content data for first column heading

Previewing Your Table

Any time you add anything significant to your Web page—especially if you're really excited about the way it will look—take a moment to preview your work in the Web browser.

Otherwise, you might add all sorts of great-looking tables and then find that they look really strange when viewed online. An ounce of prevention, as they say, is worth a pound of cure.

Preview Your Table

① Click the Preview in Browser tool in the Common toolbar.

② Click the browser configuration in which you want to view the page.

Tip

Help! My table is wider than my Web page. If you preview your table and find that it extends beyond the margin of your page, you can do one of two things: widen the page, or reduce the size of the table. The simplest fix is to modify the table. Display the page in Expression Web. Right-click in the table, click Table Properties, and make sure the Specify Width setting is set to no more than 100 percent. Click OK, save the page, and preview again. Everything should line up nicely this time.

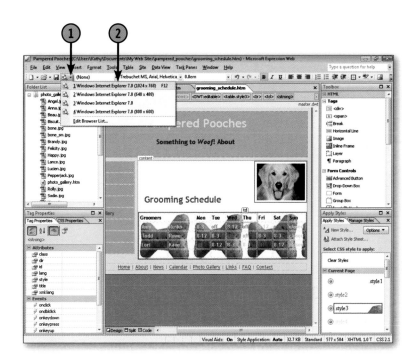

Moving On

This section introduced you to all things structure—the organic, wonderful table. The next section takes your new table talents to another level by showing you how to design and create Web forms for your pages.

9

Working with Frames

To frame or not to frame, that is the question.

For some reason, people seem to either love or hate frames. (It's kind of like mustard—you either really like it or you really don't.) Some people feel that frames are jolting and interruptive on a Web page, providing lots of boundaries and boxes for little benefit. Others love the flexibility frames offer, enabling designers to display a variety of Web pages in a single browser window.

Using frames on your Web site can give you increased control over the way you provide information to site visitors. But, there are down sides: not all users can view frames (older browsers may not have frames capability); some people just plain don't like frames; and keeping track of the different code for all the different frames can be cumbersome (for people and for search engines). Luckily, Expression Web takes care of the programming part for you behind the scenes and walks you through the rest.

This section shows you how to create frames pages, add frames, and tailor your frames to fit your site's content. The best way to understand the nature of frames—and determine whether you like them or not—is to work with one, so let's jump right in.

Understanding Frames

Let's illustrate with a simple example.

The Pampered Pooches web site design is set up with a page heading at the top (A), a navigation bar on the left (B), and static page content in the center (C). Static page content means simply that the page content doesn't change—it includes text, pictures, and links that are saved on the page itself. When the user clicks a link on the left, a new page is displayed.

If this site used frames, they could be set up so that when the user clicked a link on the left, only the content in area C would be refreshed by displaying some new content—areas A and B would stay the same.

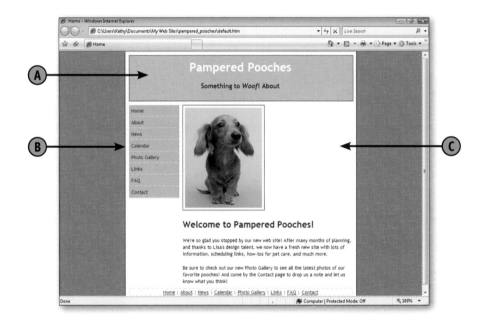

Not all browsers are frames friendly, which means it's important that you include alternate text to explain to the no-frames viewers what they're missing. Early versions of popular browsers may not be able to display frames, although all browsers released today have frames capability.

When you add alternate text to your frames pages (you'll learn how to do this later in this section), be sure to include some of the keywords you use for your site so the engines will be able to find you.

Creating a Frames Page

A frames page determines the structure of the page—showing where the different frames will go, how they are linked, and what they will do. Although it provides the basic plan for the frames, it doesn't contain any actual content on its own. Expression Web includes a number of templates you can use to create your frames pages.

Create a Frames Page

① Open the File menu.

② Point to New and then click Page.

③ In the New dialog box, click Frames Pages.

④ Click the frames template you want to use.

⑤ Click OK.

Tip

Each frames template includes a different design and navigation scheme, which means that each template page looks and behaves differently than the others. Click each template to read the description and see the preview of the page before you decide on the one that works best for your site.

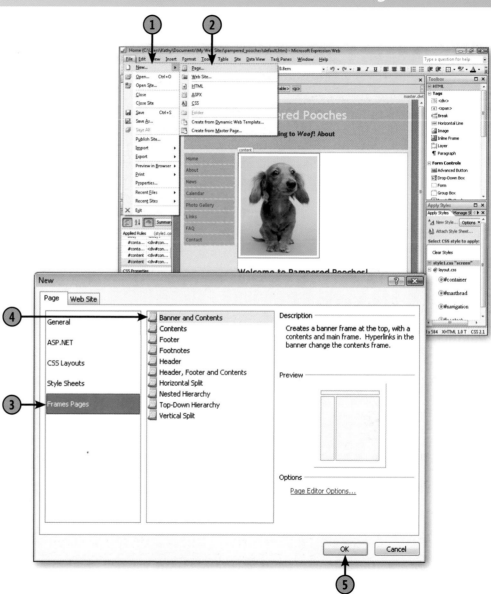

Adding Content to a Frames Page

Expression Web makes it easy for you to add content to your frames page. After you select the frames template you want to use, the frames page appears on your screen. Each frame includes two buttons: Set Initial Page and New Page. You use Set Initial Page to use an existing page in the frame or New Page to create new page content for the selected frame.

Banner frame

Contents frame

Click to add an existing page to this frame

Click to add a new page to this frame

Main frame

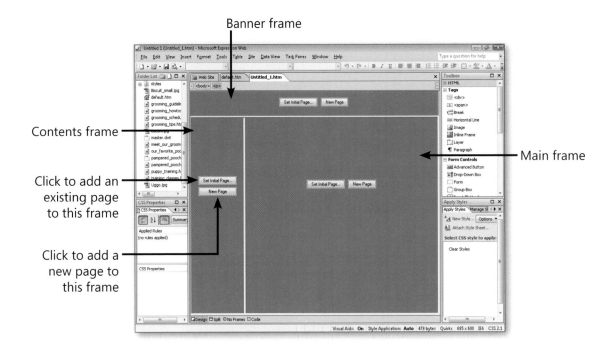

Add an Existing Page

(1) In the frames page, click Set Initial Page in one of the frames.

(2) In the Insert Hyperlink dialog box, choose whether you want to look in the Current Folder, Recently Browsed Pages, or Recent Files.

(3) Select the file you want to use.

(4) Click OK.

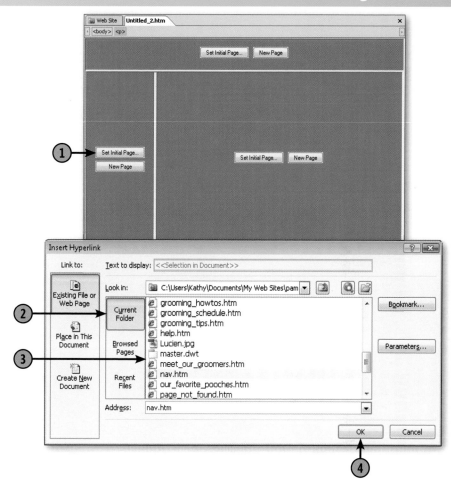

Tip

You can also add a page to a frame by dragging the page you want from the Folder List and releasing it in the frame where you want it to appear.

Tip

Did you add the wrong page to the frame? Simply press Ctrl+Z to undo the operation.

Tip

Do any necessary editing of pages before you click Set Initial Page to add the page to the frame. For example, if you want to use the navigation panel of one page in the contents area of your frames page, create a page that includes only that navigation panel and then load that page into the frame using Set Initial Page.

Create a New Page

① Click New Page on one of the frames to add fresh content to that frame.

② Add pictures and text as normal.

Tip

If you want to change the background color of a new page you add in a frame, open the Format menu and click Background. In the Colors area of the Formatting tab, click the Background arrow and choose the color you want to apply to the background of the frame. Click OK to make the change.

Tip

You can easily change the page you display in a frame. Right-click the frame you want to change and click Frame Properties. Click in the Initial Page box and type the path to the page you want to use. Click OK, and Expression Web loads the replacement page into the frame.

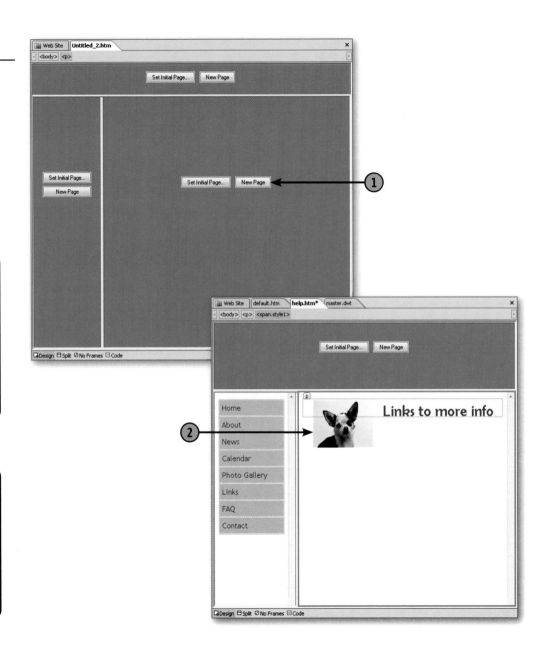

Saving the Frames Page

Once you add and/or create the pages you want to use in each of the frames, you need to save the page. This is a little more complex than a traditional save-the-page operation, because the frames layout actually pulls together content from three or more separate pages. Expression Web keeps it all straight, though, by presenting the Save As dialog box to you multiple times so that you can save each of the individual pages in your frames page.

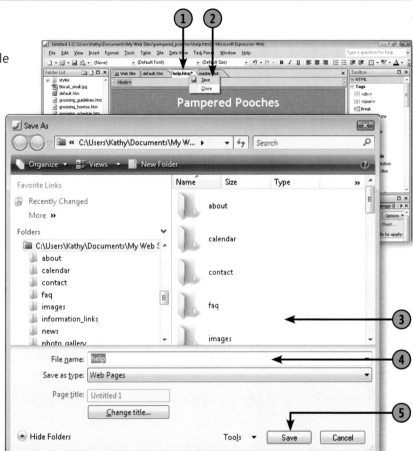

Save the Page

1. Right-click the page tab.
2. Click Save.
3. In the Save As dialog box, choose a site or folder where you want to save the file.
4. Type a name for the page.
5. Click Save.

Tip

Expression Web asks you to provide the folder and name for the file for each page in the frames page only the first time you save the content. After that point, the links to the files are established, and the program automatically updates the pages that provide content for the frames when you save the page.

Tip

You can save one of your frames as a separate page by clicking the frame, opening the Format menu, and pointing to Frames. Click Save Page or Save Page As to save the page. You know the rest of the drill: if you choose Save As, select the folder, type a name, and click Save.

Viewing Frames in Code

Although working with frames in Expression Web doesn't require you to work in Code view, it's helpful to see how the pages come together to display the resulting frames page.

Click Code to display the code used to generate the page, and look for the links to the individual pages. Click Design when you're ready to go back to that view.

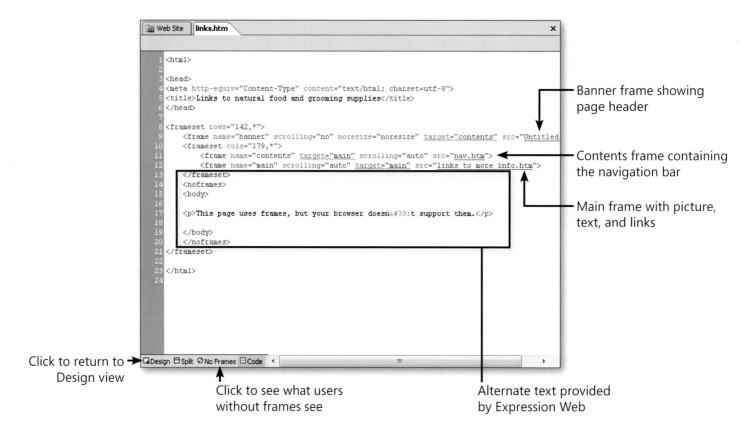

Banner frame showing page header

Contents frame containing the navigation bar

Main frame with picture, text, and links

Click to return to Design view

Click to see what users without frames see

Alternate text provided by Expression Web

Adding a "No Frames" Message

As mentioned earlier in this section, not all browsers are capable of displaying frames. Part of the design challenge in creating a site that looks and works well for the largest possible audience means that you need to plan for a wide range of software and hardware capabilities. Expression Web helps you address the no-frames problem by creating a No Frames view that shows you what visitors without frames capability will see when they come to your site.

Create a No Frames Page

1. Click No Frames at the bottom of the Editing window.

2. Format the system-supplied "no frames" line (or edit it) to suit your own tastes.

3. Add pictures and content as needed.

4. Right-click the page's tab and click Save.

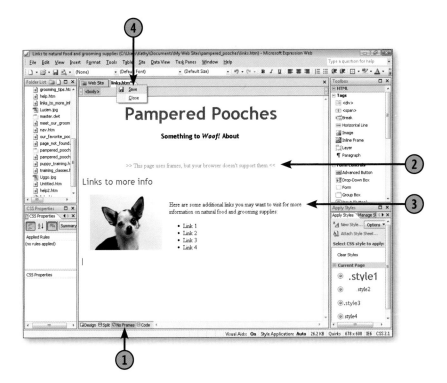

Tip

You can create a full web page on the No Frames page, complete with header, text, pictures, links, and more. You may simply want to copy and paste items from the frames onto the No Frames page. Provide all the content you want visitors to see, regardless of whether their browsers are capable of displaying frames.

Resizing Frames

When you create a frames page using one of Expression Web's templates, the frames are all preset to an established size. Depending on the type of content you want to show in each of those frames, the sizes might be fine—or they may need changing. You can resize frames easily in Expression Web. One method enables you to change frame size by using precise measurements. The other is a simple drag-and-drop procedure.

Resize a Frame

(1) Right-click the frame you want to resize.

(2) Click Frame Properties.

(3) Click the Relative arrow to display measurement choices:

- Relative sets the size of the frame relative to other frames on the page.

- Percent sets the size of the frame as a percentage of the browser window.

- Pixels is the measurement of the frame in actual pixels.

(4) Change the size values in Width and Row Height (or Column Width and Height, depending on the shape of the frame you selected) to resize the frame.

(5) Click OK.

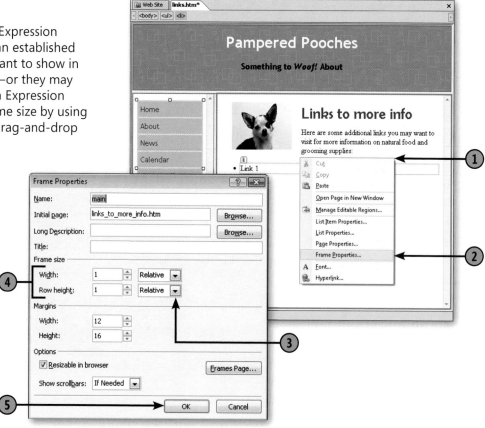

Tip

The fast and easy—and less precise—way to resize frames is simply to drag the frame borders. Start in Design view, and position the pointer on the edge of the frame you want to resize. Click and drag the mouse in the direction you want to resize the frame. Notice that the other connected frames also resize to accommodate the change in the selected frame.

Splitting Frames

Maybe you like frames so much you wish you'd made more! As luck would have it, you can easily split one frame into two so that you have even more room for embedded content on your page.

Split a Frame in Two

① Click the frame you want to split.

② Hold down Ctrl and then click and drag the edge of the frame to split it into two frames.

③ Click Set Initial Page or New Page to add content to the new frame.

Tip

If you want to split a frame with a little more precision, you can divide it in half—vertically or horizontally—into two equal frames. Click the frame you want to split, and then open the Format menu. Point to Frames and click Split Frames. A small Split Frame dialog box opens so that you can choose Split into Columns or Split into Rows. Click your choice (notice that the small image changes to show you what your choice will look like) and then click OK.

Deleting Frames

If you've decided you've gotten a little frame happy and added too many frames to your page, you can always delete one. It's simple.

Delete a Frame

① Click in the frame you want to delete.

② Open the Format menu.

③ Point to Frames.

④ Click Delete Frame.

The bad news is the Expression Web does not ask you to confirm the deletion before it disappears—as soon as you click Delete Frame, the frame is gone. The good news is that you can open the Edit menu and click Undo Delete Frame to return the frame to the page.

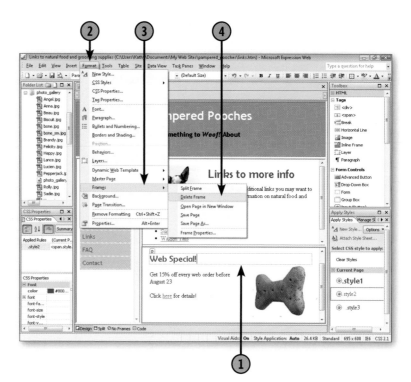

Controlling Frame Spacing

The way in which you space the items in your frame will have a lot to do with how readable it is. You can adjust frame spacing two different ways: by changing the amount of space between frames, and by modifying the amount of space in the margins of the frame.

Set Frame Spacing

1. Right-click the frames page.

2. Click Frame Properties.

3. In the Options area, click Frames Page.

(continued on the next page)

Tip

In the Frames tab of the Page Properties dialog box you can also clear the Show Borders check box to remove the defined borders between the frames. Click OK in the Page Properties dialog box, and click OK in the Frame Properties dialog box. When you preview your page in the browser, the frames will have disappeared completely and you will see only space separating the different frame areas on your page.

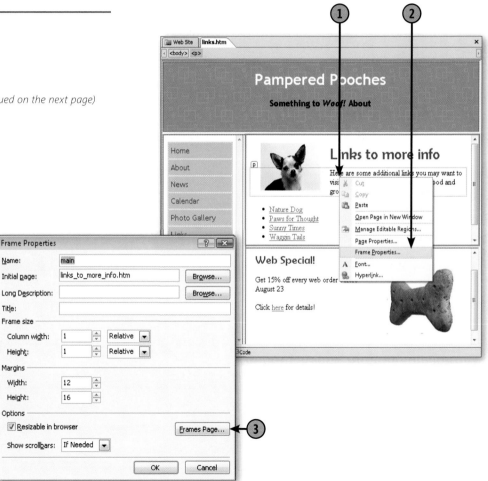

Set Frame Spacing (continued)

(4) Increase or decrease the value in the Frame Spacing setting to increase or reduce the amount of space between frames.

(5) Click OK.

(6) Click OK to close the Frame Properties dialog box.

Increase or decrease to increase or reduce spacing between frames

Clear check box to make frames invisible on the page

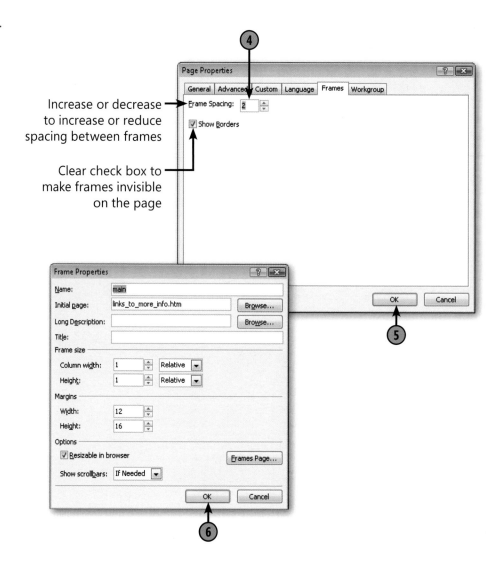

Adding Margins to Frames

① Right-click the frames page you want to change.

② Click Frame Properties.

③ Increase or decrease Width and Height to change margin spacing.

④ Click OK.

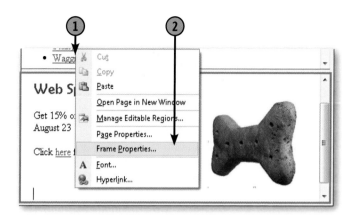

 Tip

Plan to spend a little time experimenting with the margins in your frames. You'll find that adding a little extra space improves the readability of the text. Long text paragraphs may need more room to breathe than short phrases or images.

Caution

Design view gives you an idea of the way your page will look when it is viewed in a browser window, but because of the visual aids used to help you as you work with Expression Web, it's not an exact representation. Whenever you make changes to the spacing or frame borders on your frames page, be sure to preview the page in your browser so you can see how the page will really look.

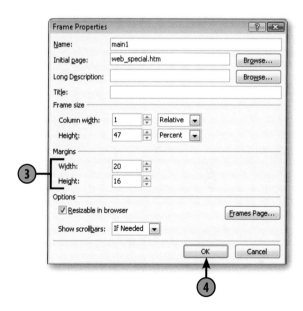

Locking Frames

By default, users who visit your page will be able to adjust the size of the frames themselves. That's right, after all your hard work, they will come along and drag the edge of the left frame until it's just a line on the screen. If you want to preserve your frames just the way you've created them, you can lock them so site visitors won't be able to rearrange your artistry.

Lock a Frame

1. Right-click the frame.
2. Click Frame Properties.
3. Clear the Resizable In Browser check box.
4. Click OK.

Caution

Remember to save your page before previewing it in the browser; otherwise your page changes may not work as you expect them to. Open the Format menu, point to Frames, and then click Save Page. Now you can preview and test out the links to your heart's content.

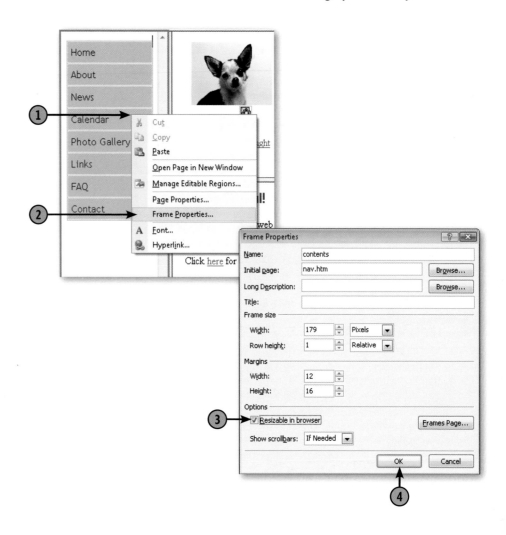

Adding Target Frames to Hyperlinks

Now that you know the basics of adding, modifying, and working with frames on your Web pages, are you ready for something a little fancier? With the flexibility of frames, you can determine what the link does when it is clicked. For example, you might open a new window, display a new frame, or display a new page.

Add a Target Frame to a Link

① Right-click the link you want to use.

② Click Hyperlink Properties.

③ Click Target Frame.

(continued on the next page)

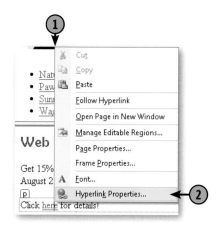

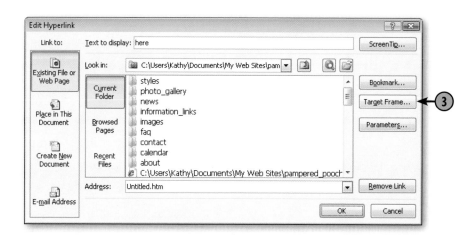

④ Click the target you want in the Common Targets list.

⑤ Click OK.

⑥ Click OK to close the Edit Hyperlink dialog box.

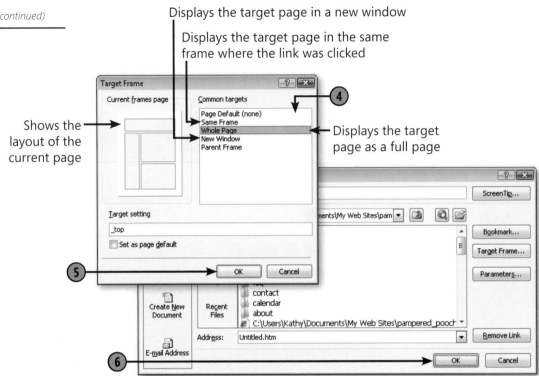

Displays the target page in a new window

Displays the target page in the same frame where the link was clicked

Shows the layout of the current page

Displays the target page as a full page

Give Your Visitors a Helping Hand

One easy-but-impressive way to use frames on your site is to create a pop-up help window that gives users more information about how to navigate your site (or what to do if they have problems). To create a pop-up help window, follow these steps:

1. Create a new page with the help content you want to display.

2. Save the page.

3. Add a Help link in a visible spot on the page.

4. Create a link to the help page.

5. In the Edit Hyperlink dialog box, click Target Frame.

6. Click New Window and click OK.

7. Click OK to close the Edit Hyperlink dialog box.

Now when the user clicks the Help link, the help content you created will pop up in a new window over the current Web page. Simple, isn't it?

Working with Inline Frames

An inline frame is a frame that is inserted on your traditional Web page. This kind of frame doesn't require an entire frames page. You can simply add the frame—and with it, the new content—anywhere on the page you want it to appear. You might use an inline frame, for example, to provide a sign-up form for a new class you're offering.

Add an Inline Frame

① Display the page on which you want to add the inline frame.

② Open the Insert menu.

③ Point to HTML.

④ Click Inline Frame.

⑤ Click Set Initial Page or New Page and add frame content.

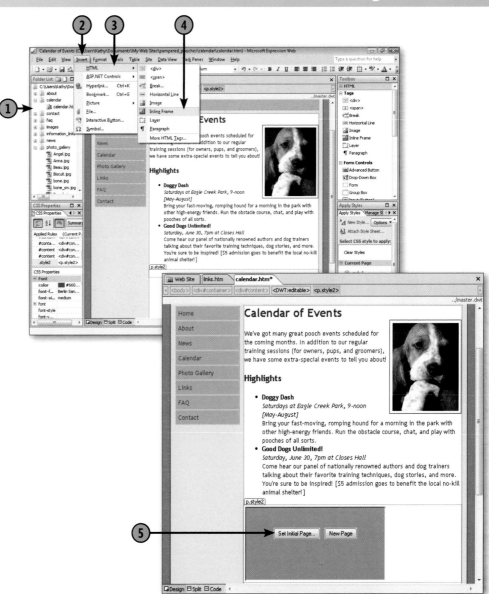

Moving On

This section showed how you can use frames to present information to site visitors in unique and interesting ways. Not everybody likes frames, but used well, they can add value to your site. The next section takes a closer look at a type of Web element you can include in a frame or place as a stand-alone object on the page: Web forms.

10

Including Web Forms

What is it about the word *form* that makes our eyes glaze? Maybe we think about what it really means when someone says, "I have a few forms for you to fill out." That *few* usually means around 12. And they are long boring forms, too, asking for information you rarely have with you. And what's worse, they ask for the same things, over and over again.

Seems like a waste of valuable time, doesn't it?

Luckily, Expression Web forms are something entirely different. They aren't boring; they aren't difficult; and they don't require that you carry a boatload of ID cards with you so you can answer all the questions correctly. In fact, in Expression Web, forms are your friends.

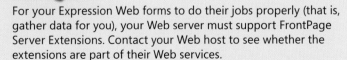

Tip

For your Expression Web forms to do their jobs properly (that is, gather data for you), your Web server must support FrontPage Server Extensions. Contact your Web host to see whether the extensions are part of their Web services.

Simplifying Forms

A form in Expression Web is really just HTML that is arranged and saved in such a way that you can use it to ask your site visitors questions and then record their answers. Their answers may be valuable data for you, if you ask the right questions. Here are a few ways you might use forms on your Web site:

- A customer satisfaction survey that lets you know what visitors think of your site

- A registration form for classes you'll be offering in the fall

- A way for visitors to vote on their favorite vacation packages

- A way for people to order a product from your site

Tip ✓

Bear in mind that you can design a form to present visitors with choices about products, but to accept and process payment online, you need some sort of secure shopping cart experience. Adding e-commerce capabilities to your Web site is beyond the "plain and simple" mandate for this book, but there are a number of great resources available online today to help you.

- An online quiz that enables your students to show they've read the material about single-cell protozoa (Can you tell I've been watching the Science channel?)

Form Terminology

Knowing some of the basic form terms will be helpful as you work through the simple examples in this section. Here are the words and phrases you'll commonly see in any discussion of forms:

A *form* is any online or printed document that has a purpose of gathering information.

The *form area* is the place on the Expression Web page where you create the form.

Form controls are the tools you use to add the fields and labels that will gather the information. Input (Button), Input (Checkbox), and Text Area are all examples of form controls in Expression Web.

Form fields (also called simply *fields*) are the areas on the form where users provide the information you're asking for.

Field values are the individual pieces of information the user enters or selects in the field.

Labels enable you to add field names to the form to let users know what type of information you want them to enter.

Input controls are the types of form controls that enable users to add answers to the form. Expression Web provides 13 different input form controls.

A *form handler* is a program that tells the Web server what to do with the data once it's gathered from your form. The form handler is not part of Expression Web—it is part of your Web host's services.

Anatomy of a Form

Form heading

Drag to add form controls to form area

Form area

Form text

Form controls

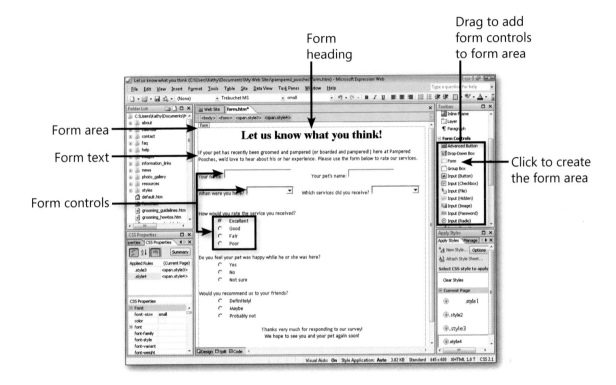

Click to create the form area

Tip

Adding a form on a page that gets its design from a Dynamic Web Template is a bit trickier than adding a form on a blank page. So for your first form, if you plan to follow along with the steps in this section, keep things simple by clicking New in the Common toolbar to create a blank Web page.

Understanding Form Controls

All the tools you need to create your first form are found in the Toolbox in the upper right corner of the Expression Web window. We're specifically interested in the Form Controls area (immediately following the Tags section). Here's a quick introduction to the various form controls, along with ideas for the way they work on your forms:

Know Your Form Controls

Control	Name	Use it to . . .
ABC	Advanced Button	Create a command button you can customize.
	Drop-Down Box	Offer a list of answers.
	Form	Add the Form area to the page.
xyz	Group Box	Arrange form controls to simplify the form.
ab	Input (Button)	Add a command button to the form.
✓	Input (Checkbox)	Add a check box control.
	Input (File)	Enable users to submit a file with the form.
abl	Input (Hidden)	Gather information the user doesn't see (for example, referring Web page, IP address, etc.).
	Input (Image)	Enable users to submit a picture with the form.
**	Input (Password)	Require users to enter a password.
◉	Input (Radio)	Give users a range of choices with one selection allowed.
	Input (Reset)	Let users reset the form and start again.
	Input (Submit)	Give users the means to complete the form and submit responses.
abl	Input (Text)	Enable users to type a response to a question.
A	Label	Add a text label to the form field.
	Text Area	Give users an area to enter longer comments.

Creating a Form

The first step in adding a form to your Web site involves adding a form area. The form area is a container on the page where you'll place all the form fields. All items you add to the form have to go within the form area; otherwise Expression Web won't recognize them as form elements, and they won't function the way you're hoping.

Create the Form Area

① Display the page where you want to add the form.

② Click and drag the Form control from the Toolbox.

③ Position the Form control on the page and release the mouse button.

Tip

You can add a form to an existing page or create a new page for the form.

Try This!

Create a new page for your form or display the page where you want to add a form. Add a form area by dragging the Form control from the Toolbox to the page. Click Split to see what the form area looks like in the code of your page. Click Design to return the page to Design view.

See Also

To learn more about using frames with Expression Web, see Section 9, "Working with Frames."

Tip

You can also create a form as a separate page and then link to it from a frames page so that when the user clicks the form, it appears in a frame within the page the user was viewing at the time. To set up the form so that it appears in a frame, right-click the form, click Form Properties, click the Target Frame button, and select the Common target setting you want to use. Click OK twice—once to save your settings in the Target Frame dialog box, and again to close the Form Properties dialog box.

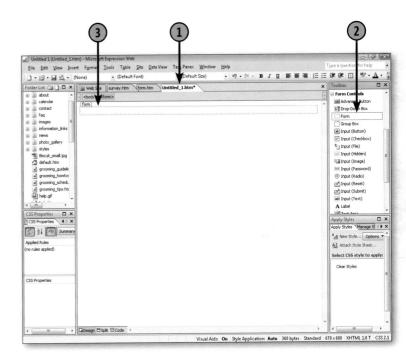

Labels vs. Regular Text

When you are adding the field names for the form fields you want to add (for example, typing the name **First Name** on the form just before you add a field to collect that information), it's a good idea to use the Label form control to set things up for you. When you drag Label from the Toolbox to the form, Expression Web inserts an HTML command that looks like this:

```
<label id="label1">|</label>
```

The cursor (represented here by the character |) is placed between the opening and closing tags. When you type the field name (such as **First Name**), it is inserted between the tags, and in that way is assigned a label ID and coded appropriately on the form. This naming process is important for data management and will assist the form handler (and any future data applications that use this information) in saving the data in a way that will be helpful to you later.

Inserting Text

Once you create the form area, you can add text to welcome the site visitor and provide instructions on how to use the form. The key to creating a good form is to be as clear and simple as possible, so limit any text to just what users need to know in order to complete the form. (Do make the text friendly, though.)

Insert Text on the Form

① Click inside the form area.

② Type the text you want to add.

③ Choose a style for the text.

Tip ✓

Continue adding text as needed on your form, formatting and applying styles as needed to get the effect you want.

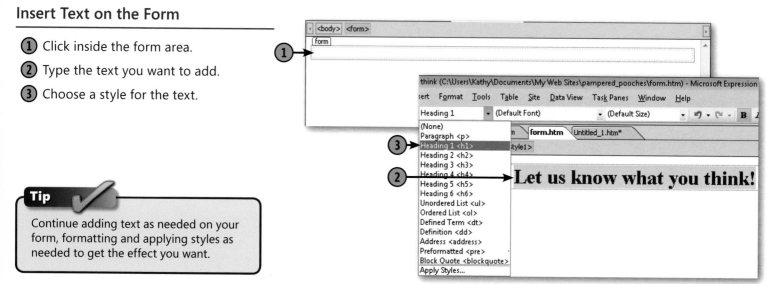

Adding a Form Control

You'll use form controls to add the items on the form that actually collect the information users enter. If you want to create a list of check boxes users can select, you'll use the Input (Checkbox) form control. If you want to add an area for a user to type his or her name, you'll use the Input (Text) form control. The area that is added after you use the form control is what's known as a *field*.

Add a Form Control

① In the Toolbar, click the form control you want to add.

② Drag it to the form area and release the mouse button.

Tip

If you have a number of form fields that all relate to a specific topic—for example, three questions about the visitor's experience on your site—you can make things easier for the user by creating a group box. To learn how to add a group box for your fields, see "Group Fields on a Form," later in this section.

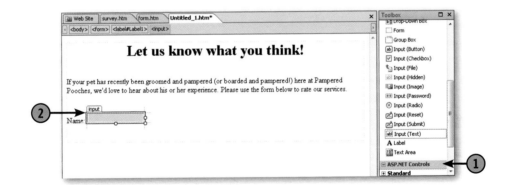

Resizing Form Fields

When you use a form control to add a field to your form, the field appears as soon as you release the mouse button. Depending on the type of field you've added, you may want to play with the size a little bit. You can resize all the fields on your form—including check boxes and radio buttons (although for most purposes those controls are probably the perfect size).

Resize a Form Field

① Click the form field you want to resize.

② Drag the end of the field until it is the size you want, and release the mouse button.

Tip

Notice that as you drag the side of the form field, the exact measurements of the field—in pixels—appears along the edge of the field. You can resize a field both vertically and horizontally.

Tip

If you want your form fields to be of a uniform length, you can be more precise about resizing them by changing the character length in the Field Properties dialog box.

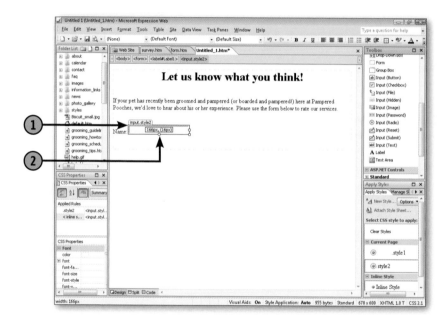

Setting Field Properties

After you add the fields to the form, you are ready to add the particulars. Setting the properties for a field involves making choices about the name of the field, any values you want to be displayed automatically in the field, and the order (in fields that offer choices) of the items presented.

Set Field Properties

① Right-click the field you want to set properties for.

② Click Form Field Properties.

③ In the Name box, type a name for the field.

④ Click OK.

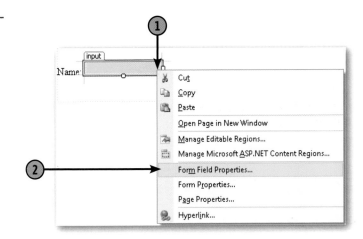

Specifying the maximum number of characters lets you limit the information that can be entered in the field

Entering a default value enables you to provide an example for the user

Requiring a password helps you protect sensitive data

Create Drop-Down Lists

① Right-click the drop-down box control on your page.

② Click Form Field Properties.

③ In the Name box, type a name for the field.

④ Click Add.

⑤ Type the choice you want to appear on the list.

⑥ Click to indicate whether you want this choice to be selected on the form.

⑦ Click OK.

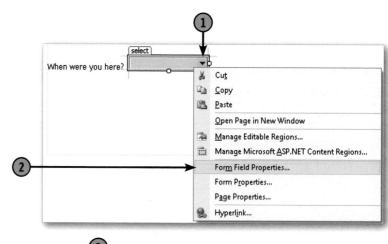

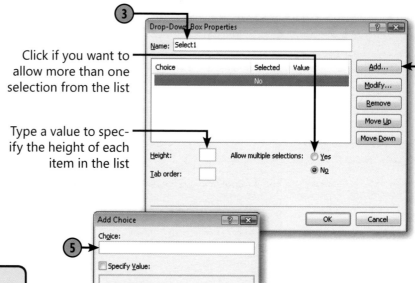

Click if you want to allow more than one selection from the list

Type a value to specify the height of each item in the list

Work with List Choices

1 In the Form Field Properties of the drop-down box, click the first item you want to move.

2 Click to move the choice up or down in the list order.

3 Repeat as needed for other choices and then click OK.

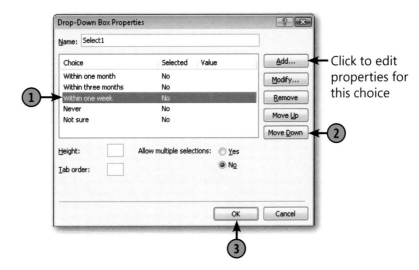

Click to edit properties for this choice

Arranging Fields on the Form

Never forget that your site visitors are doing you a favor by filling out your form. Think of how many sites prompt you for your opinion about things—your time and attention are valuable. Keep that in mind when you're designing a form you hope others will use, and make it as simple as possible for

them to (1) understand what you want them to do; and (2) do it. By arranging the fields in a logical order, and grouping fields that ask similar questions, you can lead users easily and painlessly through your form.

Arrange Fields

(1) Select the field you want to move.

(2) Drag the field to the new location on the form and release the mouse button.

Be sure to highlight both the field name and the field itself when you get ready to move a field. If both aren't selected, one will get left behind.

You can also use Cut and Paste (available in the Edit menu), or Ctrl+X and Ctrl+V, to move a field from one place on your form to another.

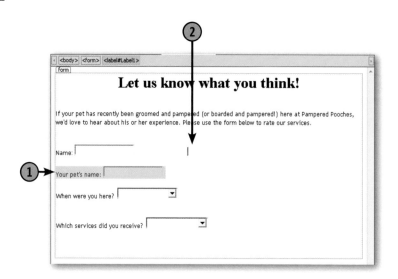

Group Fields on a Form

① Drag the Group control to the form where you want to create the group.

② Release the mouse button. The Group box appears on your form.

(continued on the next page)

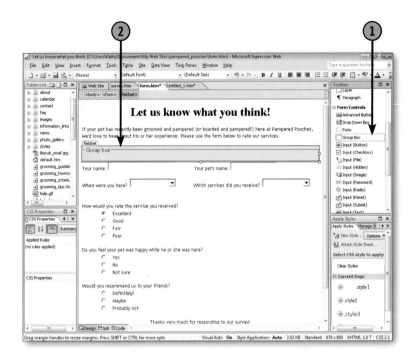

(continued on the next page)

Tip ✓

You can resize the Group box if needed by clicking and dragging one of the handles on the edge of the box.

Try This! 🖱

Create a Group box for two or more fields on your form. Drag the Group field control from the Toolbox and place it on your form. Select and drag two fields into the Group box. (If you haven't created any fields yet, you can create them inside the Group box.)

Tip ✓

Take a look at the group box by previewing it in your Web browser. This will help you check the spacing of the items in the group and see accurately how it will look when your site visitors use the form. (Don't wait until you're finished creating the form to preview it, because checking it early may enable you to spot design or layout problems early.)

Group Fields on a Form *(continued)*

③ Highlight all fields you want to add to the group.

④ Drag the selected fields to the group and release the mouse button.

Drag fields inside the Group box and release the mouse button

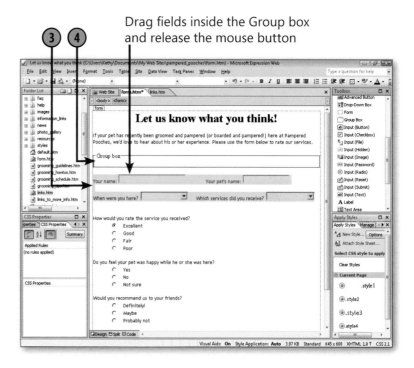

Setting Tab Order

The tab order of your form is an important thing because it will either help your site visitors move easily through the form or totally confuse them. The tab order is the order in which the cursor moves from field to field on the form. If you've ever tried to fill out a form online and found that the cursor moves to the next field *down* when you expected it to go *across*, you know that the world stops turning at that moment. Things just don't make sense. And if you're really frustrated about it, you might just click away from the form and not finish answering the site's questions.

To keep that from happening on your site, give visitors a logical, gentle tab order. This section describes how to do it.

Set Tab Order

① Right-click the field in the top left corner of your form.

② Click Form Field Properties.

③ Click in the Tab Order field and type **1**.

④ Click OK. Repeat for the additional fields on your form by choosing the next field in the order you want the visitor to follow and increasing the number by one each time.

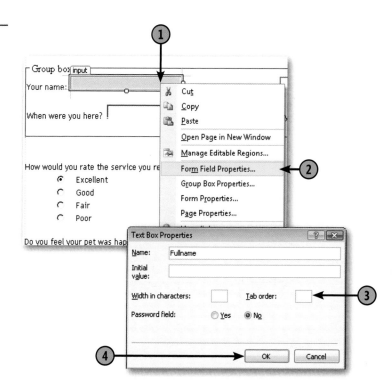

Tip

The name of the command that appears in place of Form Field Properties may vary depending on which type of form control you've selected. The Advanced Button control, for example, displays Advanced Button Properties, and the Input (Checkbox) control shows Form Field Properties.

Tip

It's a good idea to wait to set the tab order for your fields until you are sure they are in their final order. If you set tab order while you are still grouping, revising, and reordering fields on the form, you'll just have to repeat your efforts.

Moving On

This section showed you how with just a few simple drag-and-drop operations and a little fine-tuning, you can create a Web form that will enable you to collect information from the people who visit your site. (Remember that you need to have access to a Web server running FrontPage Server Extensions to use forms.) The next chapter continues the focus on the end-user experience by showing you how to add interactive elements—buttons, navigation bars, and more—to your site.

Adding Interactivity

Congratulations! You have mastered many of the basics of Expression Web and are now venturing into new territory where you can make your site stand out from the rest of the pack. Now you get to envision the type of interactivity you want your site to offer visitors. This doesn't have to be anything big—maybe it's something as simple as a set of professional interactive buttons or as funky as a podcast. This section provides you with a series of simple techniques you can use to add customized buttons, a navigation bar, page transitions, and even sound to your Web pages.

Adding Interactive Buttons

In the last section, you learned how to add buttons to your forms that would gather information from users. Expression Web provides tools for you to create another kind of button as well—a professional-looking, colorful button that links to your other pages, your e-mail address, or another site on the Web.

Expression Web's buttons are fun to work with and easy to create and change. A simple button editor is built into the program and walks you through choosing a font, adding text, selecting the alignment, and setting the appearance of the button when it is clicked.

Choose a Button Style

① Open the Insert menu.

② Click Interactive Button.

③ Scroll through the Buttons list and choose the style you like.

④ Type the text you want to appear on the button.

⑤ In the button link box, type the URL you want the button to link to.

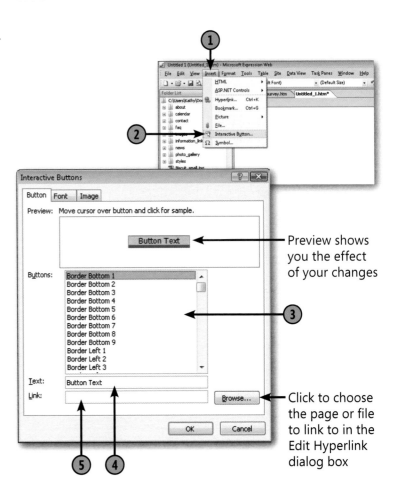

Preview shows you the effect of your changes

Click to choose the page or file to link to in the Edit Hyperlink dialog box

---

Tip ✓

Don't be in too much of a hurry as you look through the various button styles in the Button tab of the Interactive Button dialog box. There are some great styles close to the bottom of the list! And there are literally dozens of choices, so it will take you quite a few clicks to get there.

Tip ✓

If you don't remember the link you want to attach to the button, click the Browse button. The Edit Hyperlink dialog box appears so that you can choose the page, file, or e-mail address you want to choose as the target for the link.

Select the Button Font

① Click the Font tab of the Interactive Button dialog box.

② Scroll through the Font list and click the font you want.

③ Click a style.

④ Click a size.

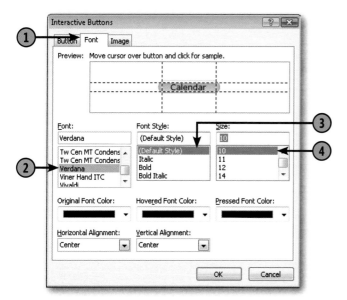

Set Button States

① Click the Original Font Color arrow and click the color you want to use for the button text.

② Click the Hovered Font Color arrow and click a color.

③ Choose a color for Pressed Font Color.

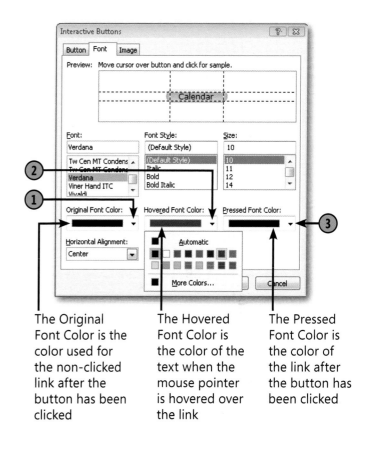

The Original Font Color is the color used for the non-clicked link after the button has been clicked

The Hovered Font Color is the color of the text when the mouse pointer is hovered over the link

The Pressed Font Color is the color of the link after the button has been clicked

Enhance the Button Image

① Click the Image tab of the Interactive Button dialog box.

② Change the Width and Height to the size you want for the button.

③ Click to save the button as a JPEG or GIF image.

④ Click OK to save the button.

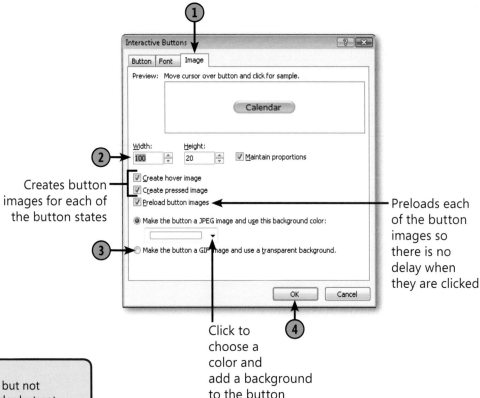

Creates button images for each of the button states

Preloads each of the button images so there is no delay when they are clicked

Click to choose a color and add a background to the button

See Also

To learn more about JPEGs and GIFs, see "Working with Pictures" on page 85.

Tip

If you want to resize the button in one direction but not another—for example, by making the button wider but not longer—click the Maintain Proportions check box to clear it before entering the new sizes in the Width and Height boxes.

Tip

The first time you save your page after adding buttons, Expression Web will display the Embedded Files dialog box, containing a list of the buttons you added (including all the buttons for the various states). Click OK to save the files.

See Also

When might you want to add a background to a button? If you are creating a navigation bar or panel, you could create a nice effect by adding a background color that complements the color of your page. Then the buttons (in yet another color that goes along with the scheme) will look as through they are standing out from the colored background. (For more about creating a navigation bar, see "Creating a Navigation Bar" on page 191.)

Creating Custom Buttons

Expression Web's interactive button-building tool is a great feature, especially when you want to create your own navigation bars. But what if you want to create an artsier kind of button, something that uses an image, symbol, or icon that you already have saved on your computer? You can easily create your own button and link it to wherever you want it to go. Here's the quick process:

1. Add the image you want to use for the button to your page by dragging it from the Folder List or opening the Insert menu, pointing to Picture, and clicking From File. Navigate to the folder you need, click the image, and click Open.

2. Display the Pictures toolbar by opening the View menu, pointing to Toolbars, and selecting Pictures.

3. With the image selected, click Bevel in the Pictures toolbar. A shadow is added to the image, making it appear to stand out from the page.

4. Use the editing tools in the Pictures toolbar to fine-tune the image, changing color, brightness, and rotation as needed.

5. Click the Rectangular Hotspot tool (or the Oval or Polygonal Hotspot tool if those better match the shape of the image) and drag a hotspot over the image.

6. In the Insert Hyperlink dialog box, choose or type the page, file, or e-mail address to which you want to link the button. Click OK.

7. Save the page and then test out your new custom button by previewing it in your Web browser.

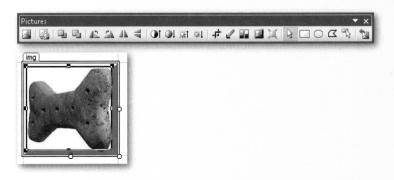

Viewing the Button Code

Even though Expression Web does the programming work for you when you add buttons to your page, you can easily recognize the code for an interactive button. It's a good idea to know where to find the code in case you copy and paste buttons and they begin acting strangely. If you are familiar with the code, you can do a little tweaking on your own as you try to solve the problem. (Of course, you can always simply delete the misbehaving button and create a new one because the process is so simple.)

View Button Code

1. Select the button.

2. Click Split.

3. Review the code in the top panel of the window.

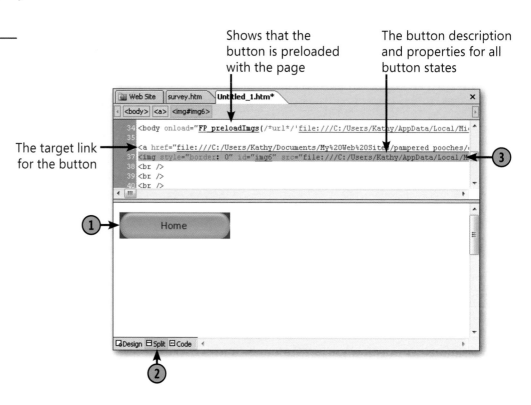

Shows that the button is preloaded with the page

The button description and properties for all button states

The target link for the button

Creating a Navigation Bar

Put a collection of buttons together and you have a navigation bar—that series of tabs, buttons, or text links that stretches across the top, bottom, or side of one or more pages in your Web site. One of the great things about a good navigation bar is that in a single glance your visitors will learn all kinds of things from its design and functionality:

- The font you use lets them know something about the tone of your site.

- The colors communicate a feeling—upbeat, elegant, serious.

- The button names teach them the basic layout of your site.

- The order of the buttons show what you think is important for them to know.

- The fact that you have a navigation bar shows that you care about whether they can get around on your site easily.

Do's and don't for navigation bars

- Don't be afraid to experiment with the placement of your navigation bar.

- Do be consistent on all pages in your site.

- Don't make the buttons (or links) any larger than you have to.

- Do visit other sites to find navigation bars you like.

- Do choose colors that stand out but complement your page.

- Do place the bar somewhere expected—on the top, side, or bottom of the page.

- Do position the navigation bar where others will see it easily.

Tip

Place the navigation bar "above the fold." When a site visitors displays your home page, he or she will most likely see only a portion of the page—the top half—at first glance. For this reason, make sure that your navigation panel or bar is somewhere easy to see that is within that first page of information. Visitors may or may not scroll down to find any additional information (let's hope your content is compelling enough to keep them interested), but they always need to be able to know how to navigate your site. Remember that if visitors get confused, they click away.

Create a Navigation Bar

① Right-click the button you want to use as the navigation bar.

② Click Copy.

③ Right-click anywhere on the page and click Paste.

④ Double-click the copied button.

⑤ Type a some new text for the button.

⑥ Enter the target link for the button.

⑦ Click OK.

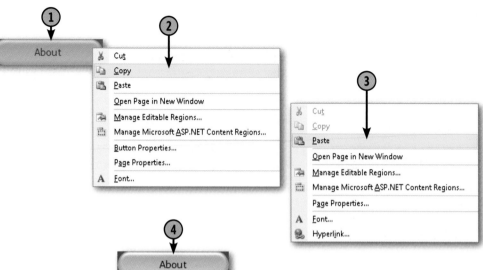

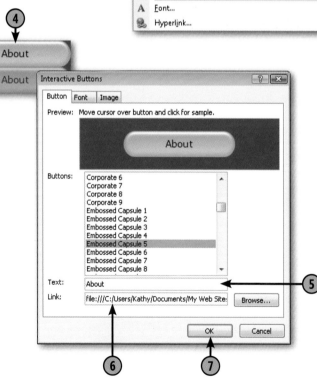

Tip

Continue copying, pasting, and modifying buttons until you have created one button for each page in your site. Arrange the buttons horizontally, for a navigation bar, or vertically, for a navigation panel.

Tip

Most designers disable the hover effect on buttons that appear on their own pages. For example, when you have copied the navigation bar to the About page, right-click the About button, choose Button Properties, and click the Font tab of the Interactive Button dialog box. Set the Hovered Font Color to be the same color as the Original Font Color. This helps reminds your visitors where they are on your site.

Applying Page Transitions

Here's where Expression Web meets Microsoft PowerPoint. This is an exciting feature if you want to add a little something extra—and something other programs rarely do—to your Web site. You can apply page transitions to your site so users see fades, wipes, box in, box out—all the fancy stuff—as they enter or leave your site, or move to other pages within the site.

Tip

Like other special effects on the Web, with page transitions, a little goes a long way. Resist the temptation to add transitions to every page—if your users have to sit and wait for your page to appear, chances are they will click away to another site.

Transitions for Page Events

Event	Description
Page Enter	The transition is applied as the page appears on the visitor's monitor.
Page Exit	The transition appears when the user clicks to move to another page.
Site Enter	The transition appears when the visitor first arrives at your site.
Site Exit	The transition is applied when the user clicks to leave the site.

Add a Page Transition

① Open the Format menu.

② Click Page Transition.

(continued on the next page)

Tip

Don't drag out the transition or your site visitors will wonder what you're up to. Just make it quick—2 to 4 seconds, tops—so they can think, "Oh, that was cool," and then go on enjoying the content on your site.

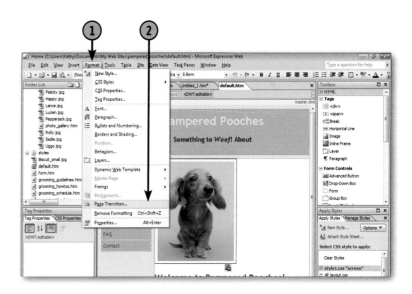

Add a Page Transition (continued)

③ Choose the Event you want to apply the transition to.

④ Click the Transition effect you want.

⑤ Click in the Duration box and type the number of seconds you want the transition to last.

⑥ Click OK.

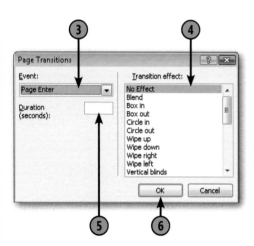

Tip ✓

Be sure to test the transitions by previewing them in your Web browser. Pay attention to the amount of time each transition takes and change the Duration setting in the Page Transition dialog box if needed.

Adding Sound to Your Pages

Let's start this section with a caution: adding sound to your Web page is a bit risky. It's risky because some people really, really don't like it when Web sites start playing songs all on their own. It's also risky because sometimes people surf the Web at work and when "Down on Main Street" starts playing on the background of your site suddenly all their cubicle mates know they aren't really working.

But there are times when sound can really add to the user experience on your site. You might want to play a jingle that's associated with your group, or perhaps post links to audio interviews, podcasts, and more. The following table lists the media file types that you can add to Expression Web.

Media Files and Expression Web

File Type	Extension	Description
AIFF files	.aif (.aifc, .aiff)	Standard sound file used on Apple computers.
AU files	.au, .snd	A sound format for Unix-based computers.
Midi files	.mid	A format designed to communicate musical information between instruments.
RealAudio	.ram	A format designed by RealAudio for streaming over the Web.
Wave files	.wav	Standard sound files used on Windows PCs.

Caution !

You can find sound files available online for little or no cost, but be sure to download files only from reputable sites (and use your anti-virus software on anything you download before you use the file or add it to your site).

Add a Sound

1. Right-click the page where you want to add the sound.

2. Click Page Properties.

3. In the General tab, click Browse.

4. In the Background Sound dialog box, navigate to the folder where the file is stored.

5. Select the file.

6. Click Open.

7. Click OK.

Caution

Not all browsers support the <bgsound> HTML tag that Expression Web adds to the code when you add a looping sound to the page.

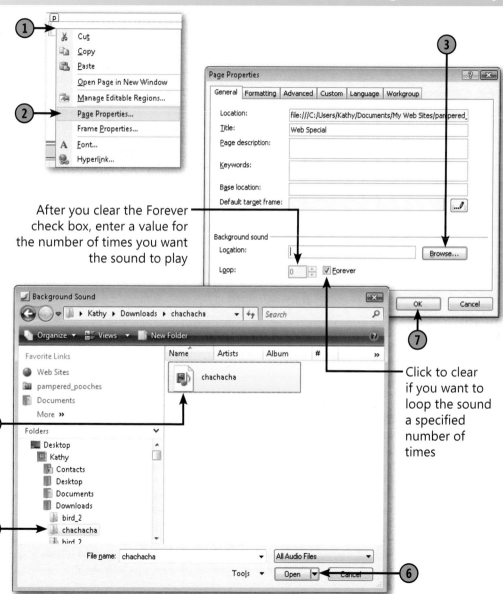

After you clear the Forever check box, enter a value for the number of times you want the sound to play

Click to clear if you want to loop the sound a specified number of times

Expression Web Behaviors

If you want to push the envelope of your technical expertise, you can experiment with Expression Web behaviors. You use behaviors to make something happen in response to an action the user takes on your site. For example, suppose that you have posted a picture of your newest product on your site. When the user hovers the mouse over the picture, a pop-up box appears, giving more information about the product. The event (the user hovering the mouse) and the action (the pop-up box appearing) together make up the behavior.

Behaviors are javascript segments, which means behaviors aren't for the faint-hearted. But with a little practice, you'll find that it's not difficult to add special touches to special items on your site. To get started with behaviors, display the Behaviors task pane (open the Task Panes menu and click Behaviors), and click Insert. You'll see a list of ready-made behaviors you can add to your site (including customizing the status bar, playing a sound, and creating a pop-up message box).

Moving On

This section demonstrated a few simple but effective ways you can add interactive items to your site. The next section takes a closer look at CSS and walks you through the process of creating, using, and modifying styles.

12

Working with Styles and Style Sheets

When you learned to drive a stick-shift, if your experience was like mine, it was probably not a smooth start. You made the car lurch forward and then stall about 20 times before you started catching on. There was so much to learn! You had to work your feet and hands and mind all at once. Oh, *and* make the car move more than 24 inches at a time.

Learning CSS is a little like figuring out how to shift gears. It's really not a hugely difficult thing—it's just a bit challenging at first. The best way to learn CSS is to begin working with it, a bit at a time. In fact, as you'll see in this section, Expression Web has been helping you all along, by creating styles while you work. By the end of this section, you'll know where those styles came from, where they go, and how you can use them to make your tasks easier in Expression Web.

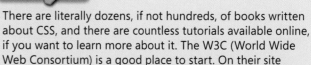

Tip

There are literally dozens, if not hundreds, of books written about CSS, and there are countless tutorials available online, if you want to learn more about it. The W3C (World Wide Web Consortium) is a good place to start. On their site (*www.w3c.org*), you'll find tutorials, specifications, and more.

CSS Basics

Visit any site, read any article, or pick up any book about Web design and you're going to see the acronym *CSS* peppered throughout its pages. CSS stands for *Cascading Style Sheets* and refers to a method of controlling the display of your Web page content. Here are some quick facts about CSS to help you understand the basics:

- CSS is commonly used both as a term for the technology (applying styles to Web page elements) and as a reference to an actual style sheet that you may or may not attach to your page.

- Cascading Style Sheets enable you to control the format of the items displayed on your Web pages.

- Cascading Style Sheets may actually be a separate sheet, called an external style sheet, which is attached to your Web page.

- CSS makes it easy for you to reuse styles so you don't have to specify your formatting choices every time you use an item in your site.

- You can save and reuse CSS, making formatting more efficient and easier than ever.

- Embedded styles are CSS styles that are listed in the <head> section of your Web page.

- External style sheets are CSS styles saved in a document that is then attached to one or many Web pages.

- Inline styles are styles that control the way the selected element is displayed.

- CSS is fairly easy to review and understand; you'll get a chance to do this later in this section.

Tip

When you create a site based on a Dynamic Web Template, the master.dwt contains a full set of styles, ready to style the content you add. Click in the default.htm page to position the cursor of the site and then scroll through the CSS Styles list in the Manage Styles task pane to get an idea of the styles at work in the current page.

In short, CSS is basically what it sounds like—a list of style instructions, saved in a sheet, added to the top of the Web page, attached to the file, or inserted for specific elements at the point they occur on the page. The instructions tell the Web browser how to display your Web page, so the largest possible audience sees your site just the way you hoped.

Learning Style-ish Lingo

This term . . .	Means . . .
Embedded	A style defined in the code at the top of your Web page.
Inline	A style applied to a particular element you select on the page.
External	A style sheet saved in a separate file and attached to your Web page.
Cascading	A term reflecting how the different styles work together to provide both function and flexibility in content display.
Style sheet	A document containing the styles to be used in displaying Web page content.
Style	A set of instructions that describe the way a particular element is to be displayed.

A Simple Example of CSS

So now you know that basically, CSS tells the browser how to style what you include on your page. You can generally think of this as a three-step process:

① You type content on your Web page: **New Puppies Born January 12!**

② You apply the Heading 3 style to the text by clicking the Style arrow in the Common toolbar and selecting the style from the list. If you look at the line in Code view, you will see that the action inserts the HTML tag <h3></h3>before and after the text. You decide you want to change the format a little by choosing a new font and color for the text.

③ Expression Web creates a new style based on the formatting choices you selected. The CSS style applied to the <h3> tag tells the browser, "This style needs to be displayed in the Georgia font family, in such-and-such a size; and such-and-such a color."

② New style applied to text

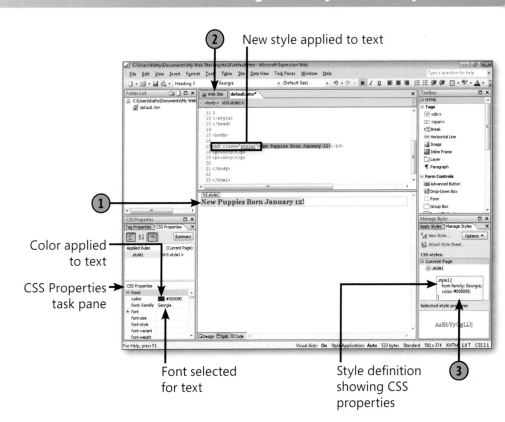

Color applied to text

CSS Properties task pane

Font selected for text

Style definition showing CSS properties

Tip ✔

One of the great things about Expression Web is the ease with which you can change just about anything you want in the program. All the different elements are interrelated, so if you want to change the color used in the style, for example, you could change it in the CSS Properties task pane, the Apply Styles task pane, in Code view, or in Design view. No matter where you make the change, it is reflected instantly in all the other areas as well.

The Benefits of CSS

CSS enables you to separate your content from the way the content is displayed. This separation gives you a huge range of flexibility,

- CSS styles reduce the time you spend formatting items on your page; you can create the style once and apply it to many elements (on many pages!) throughout your site.

- You can use the same CSS style sheet with an unlimited number of pages.

- When you have many pages attached to one style sheet, you can change the look of all the pages by changing only a particular element in the style sheet. (For a great example of this, check out the CSS Zen Garden, available at *www.csszengarden.com*).

- CSS gives flexibility to the site visitor, as well. If users set display preferences in their own browsers (for example, preferring a Georgia font family over Trebuchet), the preferences on their own system will override the preferences in the styles on the page.

Understanding Styles

As you begin to learn about CSS, you'll realize that several different style types actually control the way the page content appears. You can think of these as going from a global perspective to a local perspective.

Class-Based Styles

Class-based styles are "big picture" styles, not applied to a particular tag, but rather describing how a page element is displayed in the Web browser. For example, you might create a class-based style called *.article* to define how all the articles on your Web site will look. The instructions in the *.article* style would include font, color, and size information. A class-based style appears in the CSS Styles task pane (and in the CSS style sheet) with a period in front of the style name; for example, *.mystyle* or *.article*.

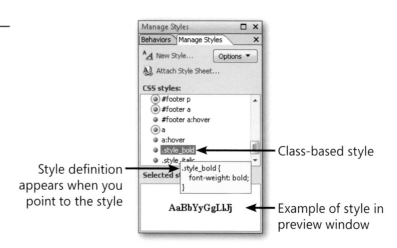

Style definition appears when you point to the style

Class-based style

Example of style in preview window

ID-Based Styles

ID-based styles are used once in a page to provide formatting information for a specific element on the page; the masthead, a navigation panel, or content areas, for example. Unlike element-based styles, ID-based styles are often used to affect layout and position. ID-based styles appear with red markers in the CSS Styles task pane, and the name of each ID-based style begins with a pound sign (for example, #masthead).

Id-based style

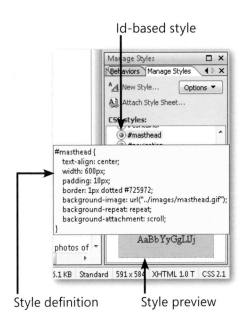

Style definition   Style preview

Element-Based Styles

Element-based styles control the display of specific HTML elements and affect every occurrence of that item on your page. In element-based styles, HTML tags are used as the style name. In the Manage Styles task pane, element-based styles are shown with a blue marker.

Element-based style

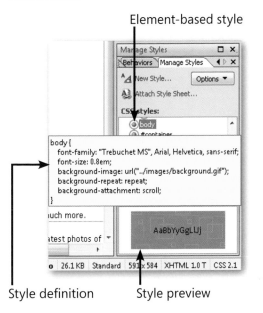

Style definition   Style preview

Inline Styles

Inline styles are temporary styles you use to change the display of a page element for that occurrence only; you don't want to save the style or reuse it in other places. Unlike class, ID, or element-based styles, which are defined either in the <head> area of the Web page or in an external style sheet, inline styles are defined as part of the HTML code for the item you want to change. The "new puppies" example given earlier was an example of an inline style.

Inline style

Style definition

Style preview

Tip

The closer to the content the style is, the more influence it has. This means that styles that are "far away" in an external style sheet will be overridden by an inline style that tells the browser to display a certain phrase in, for example, flaming orange, bold type.

Viewing Styles

You can easily see the styles Expression Web has been creating for you as you format items on your Web page. If you've created examples as you've followed along in this book, you should have several to choose from. (If not, you can create a new site based on a Dynamic Web Template and view the styles included in the site by default.)

Display the Manage Styles Task Pane

① Open the Task Panes menu.

② Select Manage Styles if it is not already selected.

③ In the Manage Styles task pane, scroll through the list of styles.

④ Click a style to see preview.

Tip

If you need more room to view all the styles listed, drag the Manage Styles title bar up. The CSS styles list enlarges to display more styles.

Try This!

To help you learn the different types of styles, Expression Web gives you the option of displaying styles categorized by their type. Display the Manage Styles task pane and click the Options button. Select Categorize By Type. The styles are organized by Classes, IDs, and Elements.

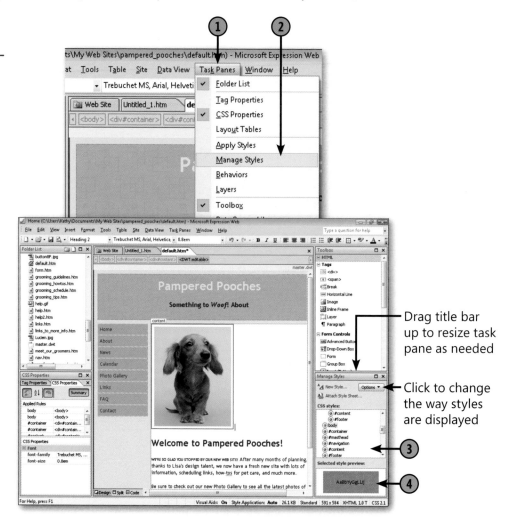

Drag title bar up to resize task pane as needed

Click to change the way styles are displayed

View Styles in Code

① Open the Web page you want to view.

② Click Split.

③ In the Code window, scroll to the top of the page.

Tip ✓

You can easily find any style in code by right-clicking the style in the Manage Styles task pane and clicking Go To Code.

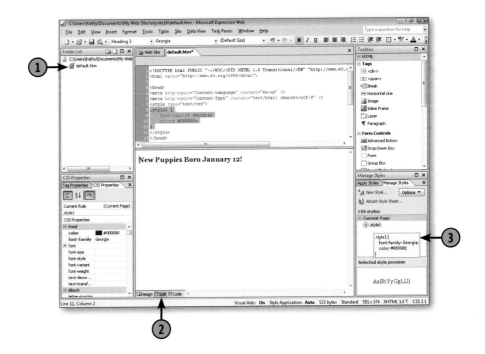

Setting Style Preferences

As you know, Expression Web generates a new style when you format elements on your page. You can choose whether you want Expression Web to create inline styles or class-based styles for the various elements in your site. To see which preferences are used by default and make changes, you use the Page Editor Options dialog box.

Set Preferences for Created Styles

① Open the Tools menu.

② Click Page Editor Options.

③ Click the CSS tab.

④ Review the style types assigned to each page element, and click the arrow to make another choice if you'd like.

⑤ Click OK.

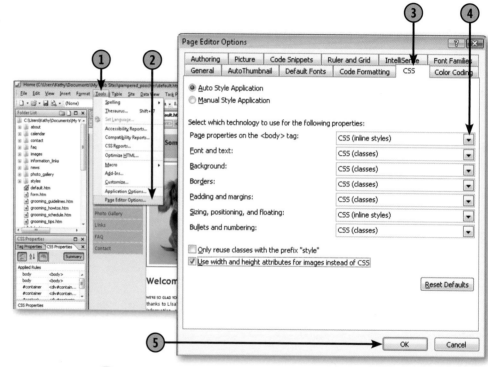

Tip

If you make changes and then want to return the settings to the default values for Expression Web, click Reset Defaults in the CSS tab.

Tip

Remember to choose class-based styles for styles you want to use throughout the page (for example, font styles and formatting styles) and inline styles for styles that you want to use for the individual elements you apply them to.

Tip

At the top of the CSS tab of the Page Editor Options dialog box, you see two important choices: Auto or Manual Style Application. By default, Auto is selected. This setting causes any style changes you make to be applied automatically to your page. If you choose Manual, the style changes will be applied to the items on your page only when you click Apply Style in the Apply Styles task pane.

Applying Styles

You've learned about the different types of styles you can apply to the content on your Web pages. Now it's time to put that thought into action. Expression Web makes it easy to apply just the style you want to the items on your page.

Display the Apply Styles Task Pane

① Open the Task Panes menu.

② Select Apply Styles.

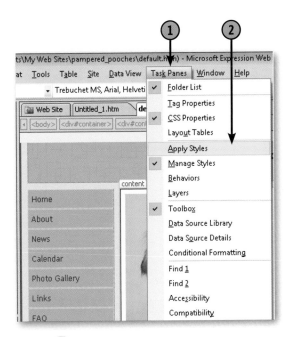

Apply a Style

① On the page, select the item where you want to apply the style.

② Click the style in the Select CSS Style to Apply list.

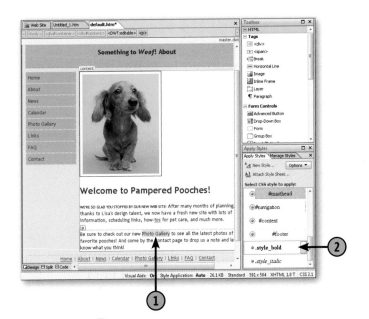

Tip ✓

If you have previously displayed the Apply Styles task pane, it may be hidden behind the Manage Styles task pane. Simply click the Apply Styles tab to make it visible.

Tip ✓

You can display a menu of style commands by clicking the arrow that appears when you point to a style in the Apply Style task pane.

Modifying Style Properties

As you continue to add to your site, you might want to change some of the styles you used early on. Instead of creating a new style from scratch, you can modify and save an existing style.

Expression Web gives you two ways to do this. You can change individual settings in the CSS Properties task pane, or change a number of settings at once in the Modify Styles dialog box.

Change CSS Properties

① In the Applied Rules section of the CSS Properties task pane, click the style you want to change.

② Click the setting in the CSS Properties.

③ Click the setting arrow, and click your choice.

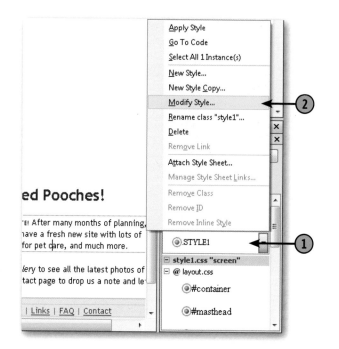

Change a Style

① In the Apply Styles task pane, click the style arrow of the style you'd like to change.

② Click Modify Style.

(continued on the next page)

Tip ✓

To display the CSS Properties by category (Font, Block, Background, Border, and so on), click the Show Categorized List button in the top of the CSS Properties task pane.

Change a Style *(continued)*

③ Click the Category of the style you want to change.

④ Change settings as needed.

⑤ Click OK to save your changes.

Modifying CSS Properties

Click this Category. . .	To Change. . .
Font	Font family, size, color, weight, and effects.
Block	Text alignment, indents, spacing, and line-height.
Background	Background color and background image properties.
Border	Border style, width, and color.
Box	Box padding and margins.
Position	Position, width, and height of boxes.
Layout	Position, layout, and cursor settings.
List	Position, type, and list elements.
Table	Spacing, layout, and table borders.

③ Choose a category ④

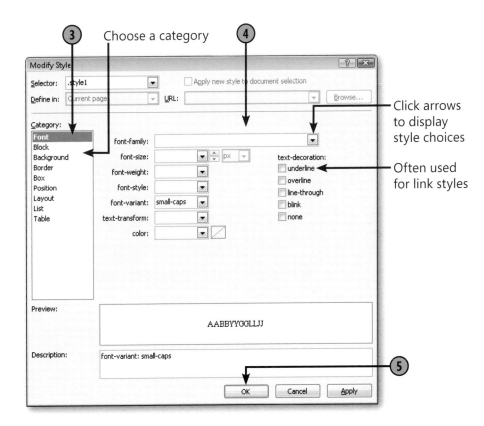

Click arrows to display style choices

Often used for link styles

Tip ✓

To modify a style that is part of an external style sheet, you need to change the style in the sheet itself. You can open the external style sheet by double-clicking it in the Folder List; make the change in the style, and then save the file as usual.

Creating a Style

As your site grows, you are likely to need new styles to apply to elements you didn't envision at the start. Perhaps you're adding captions to illustrations, or inserting quotes from happy customers. Both would require a new style.

Create a Style

① Display the page you want to use.

② In the Apply Styles task pane, click New Style.

(continued on the next page)

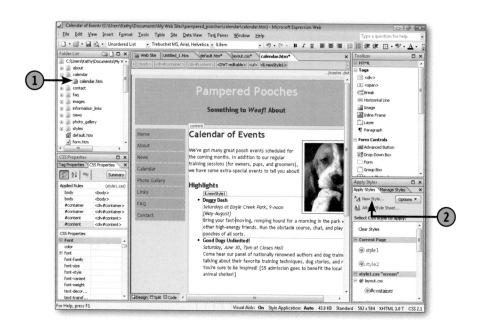

Create a Style *(continued)*

③ In the New Styles dialog box, type or choose a new name for the style.

④ Specify the settings you want to assign to the style. (Refer to the "CSS Properties" table for more info on the various style categories.)

⑤ Click OK to save the style.

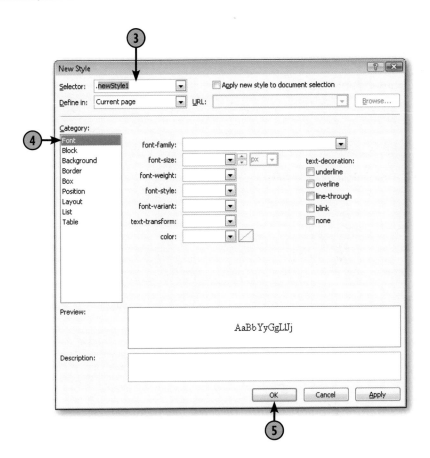

Tip

A simple way to create a new style is to make a copy of an existing style, and then make a few modifications to suit your new style. In the Arrange Styles task pane, click the arrow of the style you want to copy, then click New Style Copy. Choose the settings you want to apply to the style and click OK.

Tip

It's important to remember the naming conventions for styles. ID-based styles begin with the # character (such as #masthead) and class-based styles begin with a period (such as .style1).

Deleting Styles

Along the road to creating some really great styles you will want to use all the time, you're sure to create a few duds. To weed out the ones you will rarely use (which cuts down on the number of styles you need to scroll through to find the ones you want), you can delete them.

Delete a Style

①　Click the Manage Styles tab.

②　Right-click the style you want to delete.

③　Click Delete. When asked to confirm the deletion, click Yes.

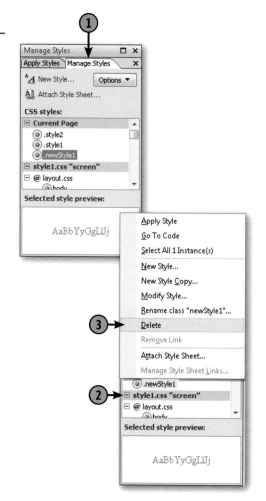

Understanding Cascading Style Sheets

Throughout this section, you've been unknowingly working with style sheets as you view, change, create, and delete styles. As you learned earlier, you can use a number of different style types (embedded, id-based, class-based, and inline) when you're working with CSS. There are different types of style sheets, too.

■　An internal, or embedded, style sheet is one that is saved in the `<head></head>` area at the top of an individual Web page.

■　An external style sheet is a document that you attach to your Web page to provide the format instructions the browser needs to display the file correctly.

Attaching a Style Sheet

Your first experience with a style sheet is likely to be that of attaching one to the Web page you're creating. Perhaps you've found a style sheet online that you want to modify to reflect your own style. Or maybe a friend or coworker designed something you want to try. The process of attaching a style sheet is a simple process that offers almost immediate gratification—as soon as you attach the style sheet, your page transforms before your eyes.

Attach a Style Sheet

1. Open the Web page you want to use and then open the Format menu.

2. Point to CSS Styles.

3. Click Attach Style Sheet.

(continued on the next page)

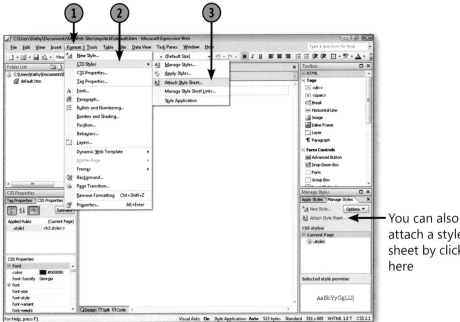

You can also attach a style sheet by clicking here

(continued on the next page)

Tip

Does a style sheet affect a page or a site? Each Web page in your site needs to be attached to a style sheet in order to display properly. If you've added the style sheet to your Folder List (by opening the File menu, pointing to Import, clicking File, and selecting and importing the style sheet), you can simply drag-and-drop the style sheet to the page you want to format.

Tip

If you want to attach the style sheet to multiple pages, open the pages in the Editing window before displaying the Attach Style Sheet dialog box.

Attach a Style Sheet *(continued)*

④ Type or select the CSS style sheet you want to use.

⑤ Select whether you want to attach the style sheet to all HTML pages in the current site, to selected pages, or to the current page.

⑥ Choose whether you want to link the style sheet to the page(s) or import the style sheet into the current page.

⑦ Click OK.

Creating a Style Sheet

You can create your own style sheet from within Expression Web and display, edit, and save it while you work. It's easier than you might think! This section shows you how to create a new style sheet.

Create a Style Sheet

① Click the New Document arrow on the Common Toolbar.

② Click CSS.

③ Click the new page and type the style information or copy and paste it from another style sheet.

(continued on the next page)

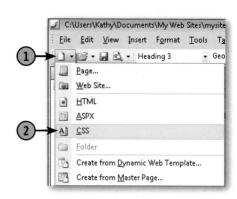

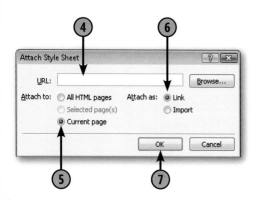

Click and type the style definitions

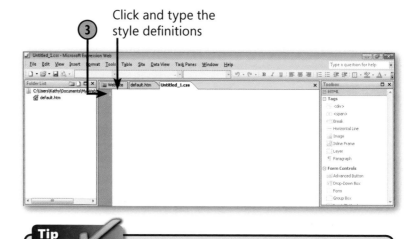

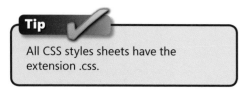

Tip ✓

All CSS styles sheets have the extension .css.

Tip ✓

Remember to use all lowercase letters when naming all files affiliated with your Web site.

Create a Style Sheet *(continued)*

④ Right-click the style sheet tab and click Save.

⑤ Navigate to the folder in which you want to store the style sheet.

⑥ Type a name for the file.

⑦ Click the Save As Type arrow and choose CSS Files.

⑧ Click Save.

Tip

This section just scratches the surface on all that's available to learn about CSS. Designers are able to create amazing page designs using CSS—and we all benefit from their talents. As you learn more about CSS, notice the different styles you like online and try to create them in your Expression Web pages. Some designers share their style sheets freely; others will answer questions if you ask. Save the sites that really inspire you in your Favorites and refer to them when you're beginning to start work on a new site design.

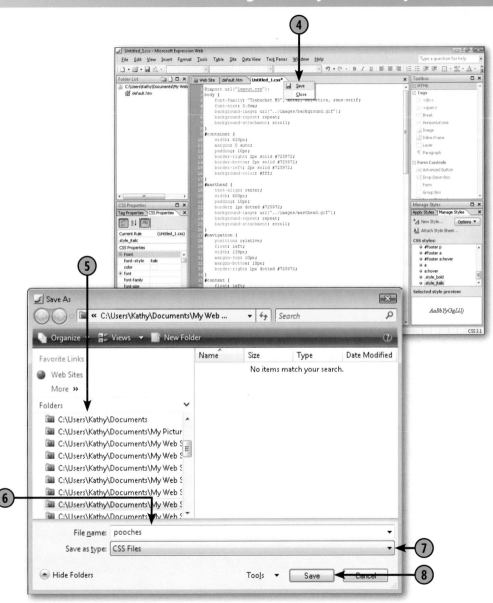

Detaching a Style Sheet

If you want to change an external style sheet that it attached to your Web pages, you need to detach the existing sheet and attach a new one. (Otherwise both style sheets will remain in effect.)

Detach a Style Sheet

① Display the page with the style sheet you want to remove.

② In the Manage Styles task pane, right-click the style sheet.

③ Click Remove Link.

Tip

If you want to detach a style sheet from many pages at once— or from an entire site—select in the Folder List the site (or the pages) you want to change. Then open the Format menu, point to CSS Styles, and click Manage Style Sheet Links. Click the URL arrow to display a list of linked file. Select the style sheet you want to detach and click Remove. Click OK to close the dialog box.

Working with Layers

When you view the code of your Web page, you will notice sets of <div> tags. This is one way Expression Web enables you to create and work with containers for content on your page. A layer is a type of container that you use to present text and graphics to your visitors. The great thing about layers is that they give you the ability to design richer pages by layering background images, boxes, photos, and more.

The positioning aspect of CSS is a bit more technical than our "plain and simple" approach allows, but to find out more about adding and working with layers on your Web pages, visit the Expression Web site at *www.microsoft.com/expression/.*

```
<div id="masthead">
    <h1>Pampered Pooches</h1>
    <h3>Something to <em>Woof</em>! About</h3>
</div>
```

Moving On

This section focused on creating and working with the styles and style sheets that enable you to present your Web content in a flexible, smart, and ultimately professional way. The next section is the one we've been building up to! Are you ready to publish your site and show it to the world?

Publishing Your Site

A little nervous? Don't be. This final step in getting your site out there on the Web is less painful than you might think. After all, you've been preparing your site for the Web since it was just a twinkle in your eye (or rather, a glimmer on your monitor). All the steps throughout this process—creating the site; adding pages; providing text, pictures, and links; working with tables, frames, and forms; and creating styles and attaching style sheets—have led up to this one moment, the publishing of your site.

Oh, well, except there are a few things you need to do first.

Before you click the button that sends your Web site out where the whole online world can see it, you need to run a few tests, kick a few tires, do a quick inspection. Expression Web includes tools that will help you resolve any potential problems before they happen. Then, after you've made sure everything is as good as you can get it, you can click that button.

What You Need to Know Before Publishing Your Site

Taking a few extra moments now to ensure that your site works properly will pay off big-time in the long run. Before you publish your pages, be sure that:

- Your content is accurate, spelled correctly, and looks good in multiple Web browsers.

- Your pictures are bright, focused, and related to your text.

- Your links work the way they're supposed to.

- Your site is a reasonable size and will download as quickly as possible.

Check Download Statistics

1. Display the home page for your site.
2. Point to the File Size indicator on the status bar.
3. Review the information in the message box.

Tip

Another way to ensure faster download times is to optimize the HTML in your site. You'll learn how to do that in "Optimizing HTML" on page 222.

Tip

Don't underestimate the effect a typo can have on your page. A misspelling in an unfortunate place ("Contat Us!") will really make an impression on your site visitor—and not a *good* impression, either. As the last step before you publish your site, run the Spelling Checker one more time—even if you've already run it several times during the creation of your site. Typos have a way of sneaking into new content. Start the Spelling Checker by pressing F7, and correct any odd things it finds.

See Also

One way you can help keep the size of your pages down—which means quicker download times—is to make sure you compress any pictures you place on your sites. For more about working with images on your Web pages, see "Working with Pictures" on page 85.

Pre-Publishing Do's and Don'ts

Do have a Web hosting account already set up with a service provider.

Do know your user id and password for publishing files to your server space.

Do ask whether the Web host supports FrontPage Server Extensions (this is important if you have Web forms in your site).

Don't leave the Contact Us link on the last page of the site. Make sure your visitors can contact you from every page.

Do remember that users love fast download times.

Don't forget to preview your site in a variety of screen resolutions and as many browsers as you can (IE, Netscape, Mosaic, AOL, etc.)

Do test all your links to make sure they're working properly.

Do include text and a link so that users can let you know of any broken links on the site.

Do remember to visit and test your site regularly to ensure that it continues to do what it was born to do.

Checking Accessibility

Accessibility is all about making sure that your Web site is accessible to as many people as possible. This means ensuring that there are alternate ways of getting your site information for those people who may have disabilities or who access your pages from other countries. Expression Web includes an Accessibility Checker to make sure your site is as accessible as possible.

Check Your Site's Accessibility

1. Display the Web site you want to check.

2. Open the Tools menu.

3. Click Accessibility Reports.

(continued on the next page)

④ Click the option listing the pages you want to check.

⑤ Select the accessibility rules you want to check for. (The default setting is fine.)

⑥ Choose whether you want to see errors only, or warnings and additional guidelines as well.

⑦ Click Check.

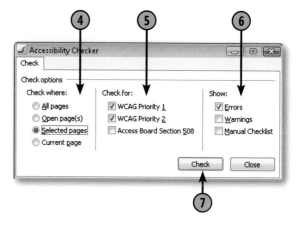

Tip ✓

WCAG stands for the W3C Web Content Accessibility Guidelines, a standard designed by the World Wide Web Consortium (W3C).

Tip ✓

When you are preparing to publish your site for the first time, it's a good idea to select All Pages in the Accessibility Checker the first time you run it. Later, when you add a new page or edit existing pages, you can run the Accessibility Checker on selected pages if you choose.

See Also

Section 14, "Creating Site Reports," beginning on page 229, covers the different reports that you can create with Expression Web. Because Accessibility and Compatibility reports are important for the successful publishing of your site, we decided to cover them here, where you need them.

Checking Compatibility

Expression Web's Compatibility Checker is a tool that makes sure that the code used to create your pages is up to the standards proposed by the W3C. The checker is helpful when you're working with content that was originally part of an older site; it looks for outdated tags that may still work but that have been replaced by newer tags since the site was first published.

Run the Compatibility Checker

① Display the page you want to check.

② Open the Tools menu.

③ Click Compatibility Reports.

④ Select the pages you want to check.

⑤ Click the Check HTML/XHTML Compatibility with arrow and select your choice from the list.

⑥ Click the version of CSS you want to check against. (The default is most likely the best setting here.)

⑦ Click Check.

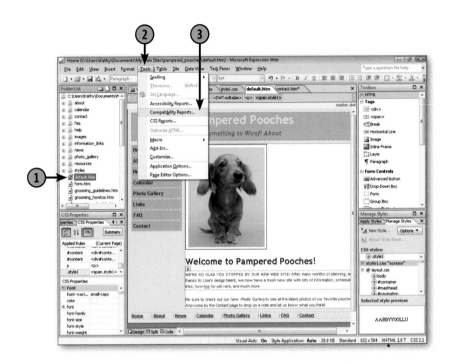

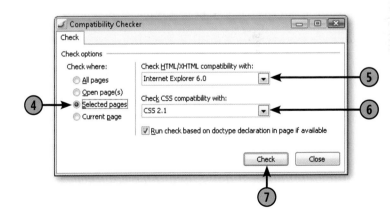

Tip ✓

The Run Check Based On Doctype Declaration In Page If Available check box means that the Compatibility Checker will check the HTML/XHTML against any value entered in the DOCTYPE declaration line in the code at the top of your Web page. That's fine, so leave the check box selected.

Optimizing HTML

When you're first learning to write code (if, in fact, you wrote code at all while you were creating your first site!), it may be a bit bloated and unwieldy. That's to be expected. You need to learn the basics about what goes where before you can learn how to trim it all down and do it efficiently. Luckily, if you did try your hand at writing some code for your Web site, Expression Web has a tool to automatically shrink the files down to include the most efficient code in the smallest possible file. This is what's known as *optimizing* the code.

Optimize Your Code

1. Click the page you want to optimize.
2. Open the Tools menu.
3. Click Optimize HTML.
4. Click the check box of items you want to remove.
5. Click OK.

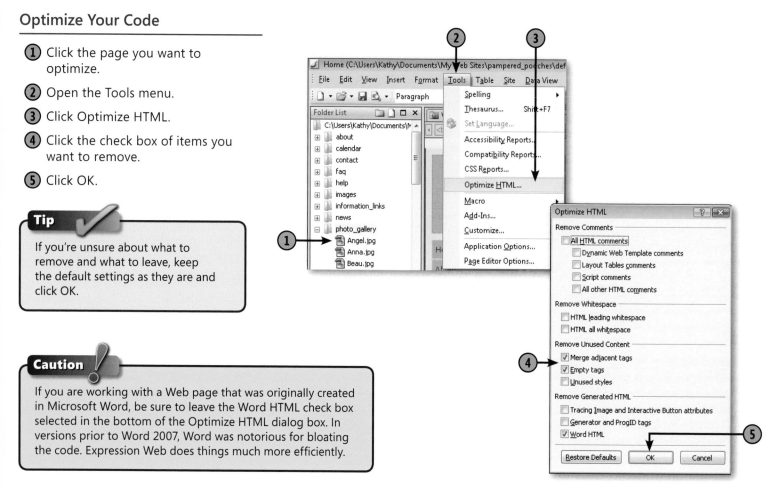

Tip

If you're unsure about what to remove and what to leave, keep the default settings as they are and click OK.

Caution

If you are working with a Web page that was originally created in Microsoft Word, be sure to leave the Word HTML check box selected in the bottom of the Optimize HTML dialog box. In versions prior to Word 2007, Word was notorious for bloating the code. Expression Web does things much more efficiently.

Publishing Your Site

Okay, so we're almost to that point where you can click the Publish Web Site button and copy all your carefully crafted-and-checked files to the server that will host your site. The publishing part of Expression Web is surprisingly easy, thank

goodness. You use Remote Web Site view to gather the files you want to publish, and let Expression Web help you with the rest.

Display Remote Web Site View

① Click the Web Site tab.

② Click Remote Web Site view.

Click to set up Remote Web Site

Click to display optimize options

Site files and folders on your local computer

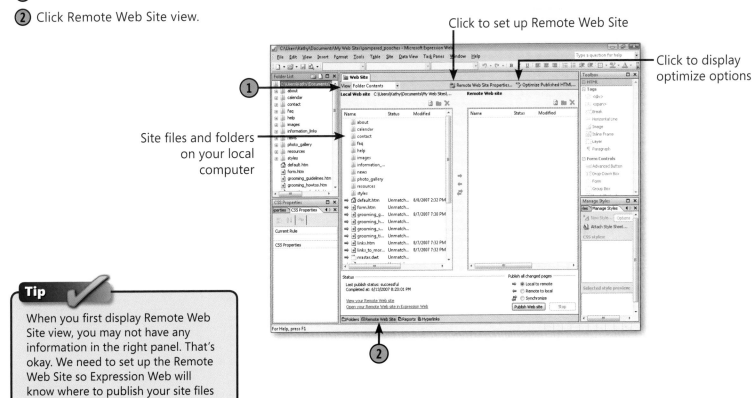

Tip ✓

When you first display Remote Web Site view, you may not have any information in the right panel. That's okay. We need to set up the Remote Web Site so Expression Web will know where to publish your site files and folders.

Choose the Remote Web Site

① In Remote Web Site view, click Remote Web Site Properties.

② Click the Web Server type. (FTP is a common choice.)

③ Enter the URL or FTP address for the remote server.

④ Click OK.

Caution

Contact your Web services provider is you are unsure whether your server supports FrontPage Server Extensions or WebDAV. If you have FTP access to your server, be sure you have your user id (or login) and password. Additionally, you'll need to know the folder name to which you should publish your files.

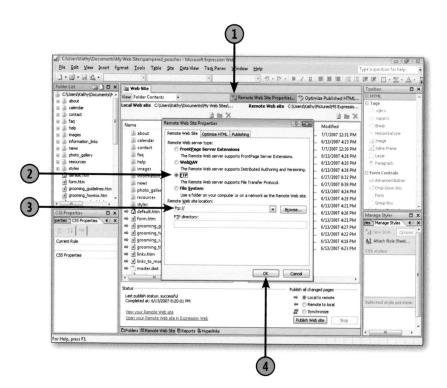

Enter Your Login Information

① Type your user name.

② Type your password.

③ Click OK.

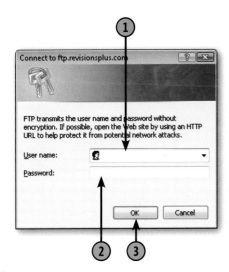

Choose What *Not* to Publish

① Select any unfinished files or files you don't want to publish in the Local Web Site list.

② Right-click the selection.

③ Click Don't Publish.

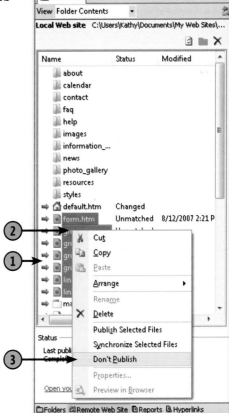

Publish Your Site

1 In the Local Web Site folder, select all the files and folders you want to publish.

2 Click the Publish Selected Files From The Local Web Site To The Remote Web Site button.

That did it! Your site is now officially published on the Web. As soon as you click the Publish button, Expression Web begins copying your files to the remote server. A small status box opens on the screen to show you what's happening. When the site has been published, a small (kind of anticlimactic) message appears in the Status area of Remote Web Site view: *Last publish status: successful.*

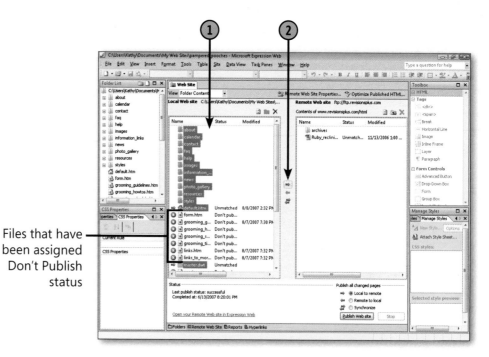

Files that have been assigned Don't Publish status

 **Tip**

This is a no-brainer, but just in case you overlook it in all the excitement: go check out your site on the Web. Test all the links, look at the pictures, make sure the text flows the way you hoped it would. If necessary, make changes. No Web site is ever really done. It's just one shade of better (we hope) than it was yesterday, and not quite as amazingly awesome as it will be the next time you update it.

Helping Others Find Your Site

You've done all the hard work—now you are counting on the search engines to do theirs. Popularity on the Web is a mysterious thing; some successes you can see coming (just look at YouTube) while others are complete surprises. You can help others find what you have to offer online with just a few simple things:

- Be sure you use TITLE and META tags in the code of every page. Search engines love them. (But make sure they really point to your content—not just to words you think will get attention).

- Write a great description that uses accurate but attention-getting words so when your site comes up in search results, people will be compelled to click the link.

- Don't miss the opportunity to include keywords in the code of your pages, and use specific, unique keywords for different pages in your site. (Make sure they are accurate, though—search engines don't like being duped.)

- Do some research and come up with a set of really good and accurate keywords that fit your site perfectly. Ask friends, family, and coworkers what they might search for. Find out what types of keywords your competitors are using. (*Hint*: It's visible when you look at the source code for the page in your browser.)

- Use your keywords wherever you can without beating the reader over the head with them. Include them in your content, your ALT tags for pictures, in links, in page titles.

- Believe in good luck, but act on opportunity!

- And last but not least, *have fun* with it.

Moving On

Congratulations! You've published your first Web site with Expression Web! It's time to send out that e-mail announcement to all your friends and family—and coworkers and customers—giving them the link to your new site. The next section rounds out the book by showing you how you can keep an eye on the huge volume of traffic (meaning, all the people and search engines who come to see your site).

14

Creating Site Reports

Publishing a Web site is a little like raising a child: your job is never done; it just changes. Up to this point in the book, you've been focusing on creating your pages—adding text and pictures, inserting links, getting everything working properly and looking good. The last section showed you how to publish your Web site. Now you're officially a Web publisher, and your job now involves several important new tasks:

- Making sure things run as smoothly for site visitors as possible

- Responding to problems (broken links, missing pictures, garbled text) that visitors report

- Doing your best to increase the visibility—and ultimately, the audience—of your site

- Finding out which pages are loading slowly and why—and fixing the problem

This section shows you how to produce reports in Expression Web that help you manage your site and make good use of the information at your disposal. Once you create a report, you can copy the report data and save it in an Excel worksheet for future data-crunching fun.

Creating a Site Report

When you think *reports* in Expression Web, don't flash back to those awful early database days when creating a report required an hour of struggling through queries and equations and data tables. Reports in Expression Web are simple, clear-cut, and, well, Web-like. You can create and display a report in Expression Web with a single click of the mouse. (In the name of full disclosure: some of the reports do require two or even three clicks.)

Types of Reports in Expression Web

This report type...	Includes these reports...	Use when you want to do this...
Site Summary	Site Summary	Display a listing of all files, folders, CSS style sheets, and templates used in your site, along with dates they were updated, publishing status, and more.
Files	All Files, Recently Added Files, Recently Changed Files, Older Files, Checkout Status	Get a sense of the files in use in your Web site, along with their ages and whether anyone else is using them.
Shared Content	Dynamic Web Template, Master Pages, Style Sheet Links	Show all files that are linked to Dynamic Web Templates, master pages, or style sheets.
Problems	Unlinked Files, Slow Pages, Hyperlinks	Display a listing of files that are not linked to other files, files that load slowly, or hyperlinks that aren't working properly.
Workflow	Review Status, Assigned_To, Categories, Publish Status	Find out the status of files in your project.

> **Tip** ✓
>
> Before Expression Web will have any data to show in the Workflow reports, you need to enter the information for the related files. You can do this by right-clicking a file, clicking Properties, and entering information in the Workgroup tab.

Create a Summary Report

① Click the Web Site tab.

② Click Reports.

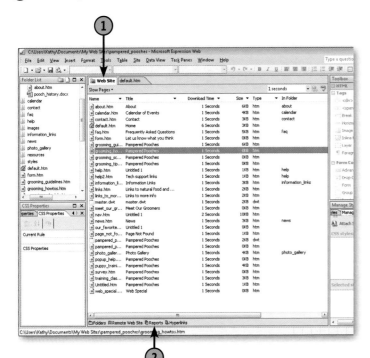

Display a Specialized Report

① Open the Site menu.

② Point to Reports.

③ Point to the report type you want to create.

④ Click the specific report.

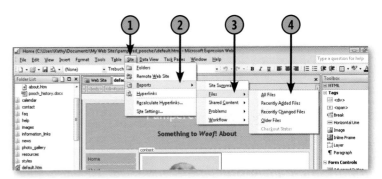

Tip

At first, the Summary Report appears to show a lot of data that may or may not make much sense. You can display other reports to narrow the display of information by clicking the arrow after the Site Summary name at the top of the Report window. A list of report types appears; point to the type you want, and click a new report.

Tip

Is the report helpful? If so, you can copy it and save it in an Excel worksheet. The section "Saving Report Data" shows you how.

Tip

Expression Web doesn't track Web statistics, although that is valuable information for you to have. Check with your Web hosting company to find out what kind of Web tools they make available to subscribers. They are likely to have some kind of Web statistics tool that will let you know how many visits your site is getting on a daily, weekly, and monthly basis. You'll also be able to see where people are coming from (the URLs of the referring sites will be listed in the report).

Arranging Report Data

Expression Web arranges your report data in default columns with Name first, followed by Title, Modified Date, Modified By, Size, Type, and In Folder. You can arrange the report information by sorting on different columns to display different results.

Arrange Report Information

① Display the report you want to view.

② Right-click anywhere on the report and point to Arrange.

③ Click your choice and the data is rearranged.

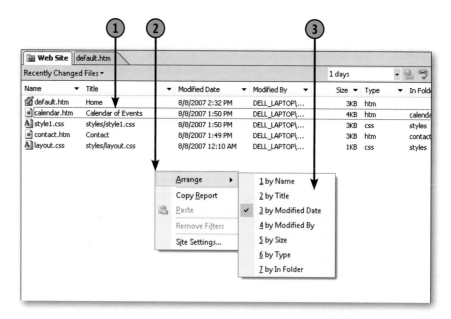

Tip

You can easily rearrange the data in specific columns by clicking the column title at the top of the report. When you click the Title column label, for example, all files in the Recently Changed Files report are arranged in alphabetical order.

Changing Report Settings

Once you create the report, you can change the way the information is displayed by making different choices in the report title bar. Different reports display different report setting options. For example, when you're viewing the Slow Pages report, the Report Setting enables you to choose

different increments of time (1 second, 2 seconds, and so on). When you're viewing the Recently Added Files report, you can change the Report Setting to display files added within a different number of days (2 days, 3 days, and so on).

Change Report Settings

① Display the report you want to view.

② Click the Report Settings arrow.

③ Click the setting you want to use to change the display.

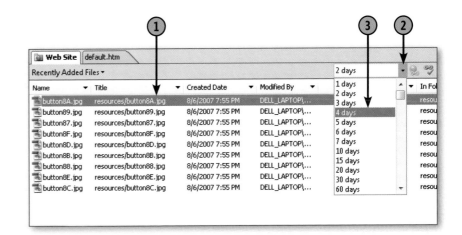

Tip

You'll notice that some reports are more helpful than others. Depending on the type of information you want most, Report Settings can help you narrow the search so that you can display the information more quickly.

Try This!

Click Reports at the bottom of the Editing window. In the Site Summary report, click the link of a report you'd like to view. Click the Report Settings arrow, and click a setting to narrow the report results.

Changing Report Defaults

Expression Web has a set of defaults that it uses to define things like what makes a "recent" file recent, and how long it takes a "slow" file to download. You can change the program defaults to reflect your own definitions of those terms so that the reports you produce are tailored for your own needs.

Change Report Defaults

① Open the Tools menu.

② Click Application Options.

③ Click the Reports View tab.

④ Change the settings to reflect your own choices for each item.

⑤ Set the amount of time you want to be reflected in the report.

⑥ Click OK.

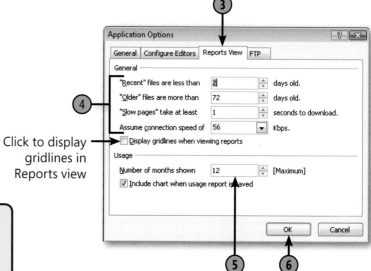

Click to display gridlines in Reports view

Tip

The default value for connection speed is 56 Kbps. If you know that your average site visitor is likely to have a different connection speed, you may want to change that value. The connection speed is used to determine what is considered a slow-loading page.

Filtering Report Data

Once the information is displayed in your report, you can arrange it to find what you need. Each column in the Expression Web report is clickable—each arrow displays a list of values by which you can sort the data. Sorting your data in this way helps you find just what you want quickly without scanning through long lists of files.

Add a Filter to Report Information

① Display the report you want to view.

② Click the arrow of the column you want to use to sort the data.

③ Click your choice.

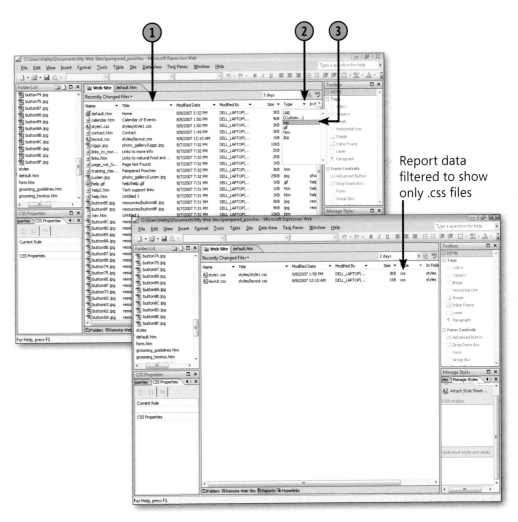

Report data filtered to show only .css files

Tip ✓

When you want to remove the filter and display all data again, simply click the Report Settings arrow and choose (All) from the list.

Tip ✓

You can also return the report to full display by right-clicking anywhere on the report and clicking Remove Filters.

Saving Report Data

You may want to save some of the reports you produce, especially at first. They might serve as a helpful resource for you if someone on your team asks a question about a particular file or a style sheet. Reports serve as a track record to show you which files you used when you first launched the site.

Save Report Data

① Display the report you want to view.

② Click the Report Settings arrow and click a filter if desired.

③ Open the File menu.

④ Click Save As.

(continued on the next page)

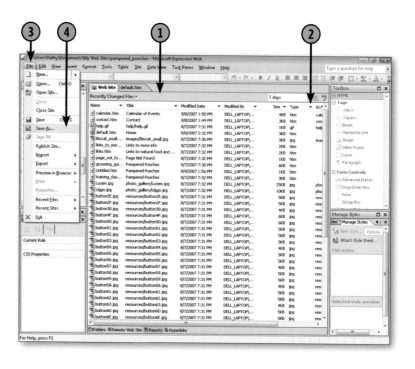

Tip

You can also copy and paste your report data directly from Expression Web into Microsoft Excel. Simply create the report and apply any filters or sorting you'd like to apply. Right-click the report and click Copy Report. Switch to Excel, click in the cell you want to serve as the upper left corner of the report, and paste the data by pressing Ctrl+V.

Save Report Data *(continued)*

⑤ Navigate to the folder in which you want to save the file.

⑥ Type a name for the file.

⑦ Click the Save As Type arrow and choose the format for the file.

⑧ Click Save.

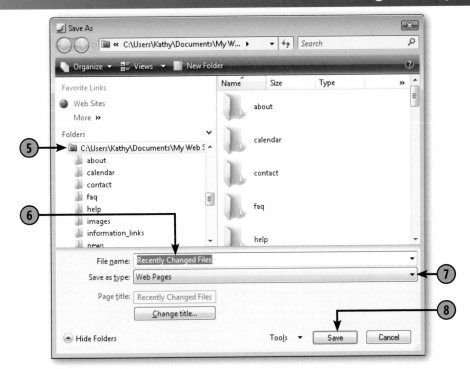

Moving On

This section introduced you to the various ways you can create and modify site reports in Expression Web. You can discover all kinds of things about your site—from file sizes to download times to which files download slowest.

Now you've been through the whole process of creating a Web site in Expression Web—from design to creation to production and reporting. You've explored all the major features of the program, but there's still more to discover! To take your learning further with Expression Web, you may want to check out these new books from Microsoft Press:

■ *Microsoft Expression Web Step by Step*, by Chris Leeds (Microsoft Press, 2008)

■ *Microsoft Expression Design Step by Step*, by Sara Froelich (Microsoft Press, 2008)

Take care, and enjoy creating your new sites!

Index

cropping pictures, 101
CSS (Cascading Style Sheets), 198–200, 210. *See also* styles
CSS indicator (status bar), 16
CSS page type, 40
CSS Properties task pane, 14
CSS Reports task pane, 14
custom created buttons, 189
custom created toolbars, 10
cutting and pasting, table columns and rows, 140

D

data
    report, 235–237
    table, 135
Data Source Library task pane, 14
Data View menu, 8
defined term styles, 72
definition styles, 72
deleting
    bookmarks, 120
    columns from tables, 139
    frames, 160
    rows from tables, 139
    styles, 210
    Web pages, 48
    Web sites, 34
description information, Web pages, 45
Design view, 17
detaching style sheets, 214
digital photos, 89
dot (.), 89
download statistics, checking status of, 218
Download Statistics indicator (status bar), 16

dragging-and-dropping text, 58
Drop-Down Box form control, 172
drop-down lists, 178–179
dynamic Web pages, 51–54
Dynamic Web template
    attaching to Web pages, 53–54
    creating new, 51–52
    description of, 11
    detaching from Web pages, 54
    displaying, 52
    overview, 29
    uses for, 51

E

Edit Hyperlink dialog box, 166
Edit menu, 8
editable content, Web pages, 51–53
editing
    links, 128
    pictures, 99–100
Editing window
    features, 12
    shortcut keys, 9
element-based styles, 201
e-mail address links, 110, 119
embedded styles, 198
embedding pictures, 88
empty Web sites, 24
entering text, 56–58
equals sign (=), 116
Export Web Package dialog box, 34
exporting Web sites, 33
Expression Blend (Microsoft), 4
Expression Design (Microsoft), 4, 90
Expression Media (Microsoft), 4
Expression Suite (Microsoft), 4
external links, 110
external styles, 198

F

fields, form. *See* forms
file form control, 172
file location selection, Web site creation, 26
File menu, 8
file types, picture, 89
files
    exporting from Web site, 33
    opening, 46
files reports, 230
filtering report data, 235
Find 1 and Find 2 task pane, 14
finding and replacing text, 81–83
floating task panes, 15
Folder list
    adding pages in, 41
    adding pictures to, 86–87
Folder List task pane, 14
folders, New Folder tool, 86
Folders view, 36
Font arrow (Common toolbar), 65
fonts
    button, 187
    changing, 64–65
    colors, 66
    font families, 67–68
    monospace, 68
    sans-serif, 68
    selecting, 63–64
    serif, 68
    size settings, 65
    styles, 207
Format menu, 8
Format Painter tool (Standard toolbar), 70
formats, picture, 88–89
formatting
    tables, 143–145
    text, 61–62, 70

Formatting toolbar, 11
forms
    components of, 170–171
    controls, 172, 175
    drop-down lists, 178–179
    fields
        arranging, 180
        grouping, 181–182
        moving, 180
        properties in, setting, 177
        resizing, 176
        sorting, 180
    form area creation, 173
    labels *versus* regular text, 174
    tab order, 183
    text in, 174
    uses for, 170
frames
    alternate text, 150
    deleting, 160
    frames pages, 151–154
    inline, 167
    locking, 164
    margins, 163
    no frames message, 157
    overview, 150
    pop-up windows, 166–167
    resizing, 158
    spacing, 161–162
    splitting, 159
    target frames, adding to links, 165–166
    viewing in code, 156
Froelich, Sara, 237
FrontPage (Microsoft), 2
FTP address information, publishing
    techniques, 224

G

GIF format, 33, 88–89, 107

global shortcut keys, 9
Group Box form control, 172
grouping form fields, 181–182

H

heading styles, 72
height
    button image, 188
        tables, 144
Help menu, 8
hidden form control, 172
hotspot links, 110, 117–118
hotspots, 100
hovered hyperlinks, 123
HTML format, 33
HTML page type, 40
HTML tags, 78, 83
hyperlinks. *See* links
Hyperlinks task pane, 14
Hyperlinks view, 37

I

ID-based styles, 201
image form control, 172
image placeholders, 104
Import dialog box, 87
Import Web Site Wizard, 25, 27
importing
    pictures, 88
    Web sites, 25–27
inline frames, 167
inline styles, 198, 201
in-page links, 111
Input form control, 172
Insert Hyperlink button (Common
    toolbar), 112
Insert menu, 8

interactive buttons, 186–190
internal links, 110–111
italicized text, 61

J-K

javascript segments, 196
JPEG format, 33, 88–89
Keyword Selector tool, 114
keywords, Web page, 45

L

Label form control, 172
labels *versus* regular text, forms, 174
layers, 215
Layers task pane, 14
layout properties, styles, 207
layout tables, 130–133
Layout Tables task pane, 14
Leeds, Chris, 237
links
    absolute, 110
    active hyperlinks, 123
    adding target frames to, 165–166
    bookmarks as, 120–121
    colors, 123–124
    displaying, 126
    editing, 128
    e-mail address, 110, 119
    external, 110
    good link design, 111
    hotspot, 110, 117–118
    hovered hyperlinks, 123
    in-page, 111
    internal, 110–111
    Keyword Selector tool, 114
    paths, 116
    picture, 110, 116–117

text, *continued*
  italicized, 61
  pasting, 60
  selecting, 61
  spacing, 68–69
  spell-checking, 78–79
  styles, 71–72
  text wrap, 95, 143
Text Area form control, 172
text form control, 172
text links, 110, 112–113
Thesaurus dialog box, 80
thumbnail views, 102–103
TIF format, 89
TITLE tags, 227
titles, Web page, 45
toolbars
  buttons, adding and removing, 10
  customizing, 10
  list of, 11
Toolbox task pane, 14
Tools menu, 8
transitions, 193–194

U–V

underscore (_), 48
undoing changes to pictures, 101
unordered list styles, 72
unordered lists, 73–74
URL information
  file location selection, 26
  publishing techniques, 224
View menu
viewing
  button code, 190
  frames in code, 156
  links as code, 114–115
  pictures in code, 104–106

viewing, *continued*
  styles, 202
  styles in code, 203
  table code, 146
  Web site information, 35–37
views
  Code, 17
  Design, 17
  displaying, 17
  moving among, shortcut keys, 9
  moving between, 35
  Split, 17–18
visited hyperlinks, 123
Visual Aids indicator (status bar), 16
Visual Studio 2005 (Microsoft), 2

W

Wave files, 194
WCAG (W3C Web Content Accessibility), 220
Web design, about this book, 1–4
Web forms. *See* forms
Web pages
  adding in Folder list, 41
  adding new, 40
  adding tables to, 134
  ASPX page type, 40
  backgrounds, 49
  closing, 47
  creating from existing page, 41
  CSS page type, 40
  deleting, 48
  description information, 45
  dynamic, 51–54
  Dynamic Web template attachment, 53–54
  Dynamic Web template detachment, 54
  editable content, 51

Web pages, *continued*
  HTML page type, 40
  keywords, 45
  master design, adding, 42
  moving between, 46
  naming, 43
  opening, 46
  pictures, adding, 49, 91–92
  previewing, 50
  properties, setting, 44–45
  renaming, 47–48
  saving, 43–44
  size settings, 50
  titles, 45
  transitions, 193–194
Web sites
  creating from scratch, 24
  creation techniques, 22
  deleting, 34
  empty, 24
  exporting, 33
  exporting files from, 33
  importing, 25–27
  one-page site creation, 23
  opening, 12, 30
  renaming, 31–32
  saving, 23
  viewing information in, 35–37
Web-safe colors, 102
width
  button image, 188
  table columns, 136
  tables, 144
Window menu, 8
WMP format, 89
WMV format, 89
workflow reports, 230
workspace features, 7
World Wide Web Consortium (W3C), 220
wrapping text around tables, 143

About the Author

Katherine Murray is the author of many books on technology, with a special affinity for any program related to designing or writing for print or online media. In addition to her computer books, Katherine wrote the in-the-box documentation for Microsoft Office 2007 and is a regular digital-lifestyle contributor to several Microsoft sites, as well as CNET's TechRepublic. Katherine also is an avid blogger, publishing multiple blogs on a variety of topics.

Katherine has been fascinated by computers since the early 1980s when she got her hands on one of the first IBM PCs to arrive in the city of Indianapolis. She still lives in the Midwest, close to her three children and new grandbaby, with two dogs, three cats, and a turtle. When she's not writing or playing with the baby, she enjoys many wireless activities, including gardening, cooking, reading, listening to live jazz, and playing *Trivial Pursuit* with the kids.

What do you think of this book?

We want to hear from you!

Do you have a few minutes to participate in a brief online survey?

Microsoft is interested in hearing your feedback so we can continually improve our books and learning resources for you.

To participate in our survey, please visit:

www.microsoft.com/learning/booksurvey/

...and enter this book's ISBN-10 number (appears above barcode on back cover*). As a thank-you to survey participants in the United States and Canada, each month we'll randomly select five respondents to win one of five $100 gift certificates from a leading online merchant. At the conclusion of the survey, you can enter the drawing by providing your e-mail address, which will be used for prize notification only.

Thanks in advance for your input. Your opinion counts!

***Microsoft** Press*

* Where to find the ISBN-10 on back cover

ISBN-13: 000-0-0000-0000-0
ISBN-10: 0-0000-00000

0 0 0 0 0

0 000000 000000

Example only. Each book has unique ISBN.

No purchase necessary. Void where prohibited. Open only to residents of the 50 United States (includes District of Columbia) and Canada (void in Quebec). For official rules and entry dates see:

www.microsoft.com/learning/booksurvey/